At Issue

| Fracking

Other Books in the At Issue Series:

At Issue

| Fracking

Tamara Thompson, Book Editor

GREENHAVEN PRESS
A part of Gale, Cengage Learning

GALE
CENGAGE Learning·

Detroit • New York • San Francisco • New Haven, Conn • Waterville, Maine • London

Elizabeth Des Chenes, *Director, Publishing Solutions*

© 2013 Greenhaven Press, a part of Gale, Cengage Learning.

Gale and Greenhaven Press are registered trademarks used herein under license.

For more information, contact:
Greenhaven Press
27500 Drake Rd.
Farmington Hills, MI 48331-3535
Or you can visit our Internet site at gale.cengage.com

For product information and technology assistance, contact us at

Gale Customer Support, 1-800-877-4253
For permission to use material from this text or product, submit all requests online at www.cengage.com/permissions.

Further permissions questions can be e-mailed to permissionrequest@cengage.com.

Articles in Greenhaven Press anthologies are often edited for length to meet page requirements. In addition, original titles of these works are changed to clearly present the main thesis and to explicitly indicate the author's opinion. Every effort is made to ensure that Greenhaven Press accurately reflects the original intent of the authors. Every effort has been made to trace the owners of copyrighted material.

Cover photograph copyright © Debra Hughes 2007. Used under license from Shutterstock.com.

LIBRARY OF CONGRESS CATALOGING-IN-PUBLICATION DATA

Fracking / Tamara Thompson, book editor.
   p. cm. -- (At issue)
   Summary: "At Issue: Fracking: Books in this anthology series focus a wide range of viewpoints onto a single controversial issue, providing in-depth discussions by leading advocates, a quick grounding in the issues, and a challenge to critical thinking skills"-- Provided by publisher.
   Includes bibliographical references and index.
   ISBN 978-0-7377-6509-0 (hardback) -- ISBN 978-0-7377-6510-6 (paperback)
   1. Shale gas industry--Environmental aspects--United States. 2. Gas well drilling--Environmental aspects--United States. 3. Hydraulic fracturing--Environmental aspects--United States. I. Thompson, Tamara, editor of compilation.
   TD195.G3F73 2013
   363.738'4--dc23
                                                            2012042413

Printed in the United States of America
1 2 3 4 5 6 7 17 16 15 14 13

Contents

Introduction

When a natural gas company offered Josh Fox $100,000 to lease his family's land in Milanville, Pennsylvania, for drilling in 2008, Fox wanted to learn more before signing on the dotted line. So he started looking into drilling practices at the Marcellus Shale, the nation's biggest natural gas field that lies under large swaths of Pennsylvania, New York, West Virginia, and Ohio. What Fox learned troubled him so much that he grabbed his video camera and headed to nearby Dimock, Pennsylvania, where natural gas drilling was already under way. His plan was to chat with the locals about how the extraction operation was affecting them, but what they had to say was more shocking than he had ever expected.

The folks in Dimock told Fox about contaminated well water and health problems, and they showed him how the water coming from their kitchen taps burst into flames—all caused, they said, by nearby natural gas hydraulic fracturing operations at the Marcellus site. Known more commonly as hydrofracking, or, simply, fracking, the process involves drilling a deep hole in dense shale rock and then blasting a mixture of water, sand, and chemicals down inside the hole to fracture the surrounding rock and release natural gas into the water so it can be captured. The technique is regarded as the most efficient and cost-effective way to tap the country's huge natural gas deposits that would otherwise be inaccessible because they are locked in layers of rock.

Fracking is the backbone of an American natural gas boom that is boosting the economy, creating jobs and energy export opportunities, and strengthening US energy independence with the lowest domestic natural gas prices in a decade. But it also uses millions of gallons of water, which end up contaminated with toxic chemicals and radiation that can imperil water supplies for millions of people.

Few people outside the natural gas industry had ever even heard of fracking when Fox was filming Dimock residents lighting their tapwater on fire, but that all changed as his personal project turned into the 2010 Oscar-nominated documentary *Gasland*. The movie—in which Fox visited communities nationwide where natural gas extraction is taking place—became a global word-of-mouth sensation, introducing the dangers of fracking to a worldwide audience and spurring antifracking legislation in several states and foreign countries, including outright bans in France and Bulgaria. As Dave Shiflett of Bloomberg News wrote in June 2010, Fox "may go down in history as the Paul Revere of fracking"—the one who sounded the first alarm.

For its part, the natural gas and oil industry (fracking is also used for oil extraction) maintains that *Gasland* is full of factual inaccuracies and that the practice of hydraulic fracturing has been unfairly maligned by the movie; public opposition to a technology that has been proven safe, they say, has been generated by misinformation and sensationalism.

Fracking opponents say that one of the more troubling issues brought to light by *Gasland*—aside from wells allowing gas to escape into aquifers and toxic chemicals contaminating groundwater—is that the chemical cocktails used in fracking are considered trade secrets, so scientists and medical professionals have no idea what specific substances they should test for to assess whether there is an environmental or public health problem related to fracking. Energy companies argue that disclosing their proprietary secrets would hurt their competitiveness. In the face of public backlash on the issue, however, the industry has reluctantly embraced a voluntary fracking chemical disclosure registry online, but critics say it does not go far enough.

Among the dozens of hazardous substances discovered in fracking wastewater during a 2011 study by the Congressional Committee on Energy and Commerce were the cancer-causing chemicals 2-butoxyethanol (2-BE), formaldehyde, diesel oil, naphthalene, benzene, toluene, ethylbenzene, and xylene. Although the use of all of those substances underground is regulated by the Environmental Protection Agency under the Safe Drinking Water Act, fracking has been specifically exempted from that regulation. The exemption is known as the Halliburton loophole because it was inserted in the 2005 energy bill at the direction of then–vice president Dick Cheney, who was the former chief executive of Halliburton, the company that invented the fracking process. Critics say that this loophole demonstrates that profits and politics, not safety and science, have driven the government's oversight of the fracking industry.

In March 2011, the Fracturing Responsibility and Awareness of Chemicals Act of 2011 was introduced in both houses of Congress. The so-called FRAC Act would close the Halliburton loophole and amend the Safe Drinking Water Act to define fracking as a federally regulated activity. It would also mandate the full disclosure of chemicals used in fracking fluids. As of December 2012, the FRAC Act was stalled in committee, and no decision had been made on its future. Similar bills had been introduced in both the House and Senate in 2009, as well, but Congress adjourned without taking action on either of them.

The energy industry has fought hard against any sort of federal tracking regulation, insisting that the practice is safe and that state regulations are doing more than an adequate job of protecting public health and the environment. Industry opposition to federal regulation may be having unintended consequences, however. While the industry has been busy fighting against the FRAC Act in Congress, seven states— Texas, Wyoming, Montana, Arkansas, Colorado, Pennsylvania, and Oklahoma—have meanwhile enacted mandatory disclosure laws for the chemicals used in fracking, and in May 2012 Vermont became the first state to ban the practice entirely.

Hundreds of local municipalities nationwide, including ninety-five cities in New York State, have banned fracking and fracking wastewater treatment within their boundaries. And in the absence of federal protections, the US Department of Interior and the Bureau of Land Management are circulating proposed rules to regulate fracking on public lands that are leased for energy production.

It seems clear that even if the industry is successful in again stopping the FRAC Act in Congress, oil and gas producers will face increasing scrutiny and regulation from states, municipalities, and other interested parties in the coming years. The authors in *At Issue: Fracking* present a wide range of viewpoints concerning the benefits, consequences, and appropriate regulation of hydraulic fracturing.

1

The Serious Risks of Fracking Outweigh Its Benefits

Natural Resources Defense Council

The Natural Resources Defense Council (NRDC) is a nonprofit membership organization that advocates for the preservation of the environment worldwide.

New extraction technologies, such as hydraulic fracturing (fracking), have allowed the natural gas industry to greatly expand drilling operations and to tap into resource-rich areas that were previously inaccessible. Fracking, however, is a dangerous process that has a high potential for polluting the land, air, and water, and communities across the country have already felt its negative impact. The state and federal laws that regulate natural gas extraction have not kept up with new extraction technologies such as fracking, and they are insufficient to protect public health and the environment. The serious long-term health and environmental consequences of fracking outweigh its short-term energy and economic benefits. Americans have the right to clean air and water; strong, enforceable safeguards are essential to ensure that natural gas extraction is conducted as safely and responsibly as possible.

Natural gas development has exploded at break-neck speed in recent years, fueled by advancements in an extraction technique known as hydraulic fracturing—or fracking—that has allowed the oil and gas industry to access previously out-of-reach reserves.

Unfortunately, federal and state safeguards to protect people and the environment from the hazards of fracking have not kept pace. As a result, this development has proved dangerous, destructive, and polluting.

This unbridled growth of fracking has allowed the gas industry to run roughshod over communities, leaving a host of serious impacts in their wake—from poisoned water wells, to contaminated rivers and streams, toxic air pollution and devastated property values in towns and rural areas across the country.

At any given stage of [the fracking] process, there are numerous environmental and public health threats.

This has to change.

First and foremost, we need our leaders to prioritize more efficient, cleaner, safer, and renewable sources of power that will not poison our health or our water. Second, we must take sensitive, risky and vulnerable areas off the table for gas development. Third, wherever gas development is occurring, we need effective safeguards on the books to ensure that Americans no longer have to sacrifice their health, safe drinking water, and property values for oil and gas company profits.

What Is Fracking?

Fracking involves mixing large quantities of water and sand with dangerous chemicals, and blasting it into wells at extremely high pressure in order to release oil or natural gas deposits trapped in rock. Sometimes this can take place as little as 100 feet from homes or drinking water supplies.

The fracking process requires considerable amounts of water, involves the use of toxic chemicals, necessitates huge amounts of truck traffic, and produces large quantities of highly polluted wastewater. At any given stage of this process, there are numerous environmental and public health threats.

It can contaminate drinking water supplies, generate substantial air pollution emissions, destroy habitat and landscapes, and fundamentally transform rural communities.

Fracking is currently taking place in approximately 30 states, without sufficient safeguards and typically under outdated regulations and inadequate enforcement. The oil and gas industry is seeking to expand fracking nationwide to extract gas from previously inaccessible sites, including shale formations, tight sands, and other so-called "unconventional gas plays."

Over the last decade, the industry has drilled tens of thousands of new wells in the Rocky Mountain region, the South, and the eastern United States. In the East, the latest hotbed of activity, the focus has been on a massive 600-mile-long rock formation called the Marcellus Shale, which stretches from West Virginia, through Ohio and Pennsylvania, and into New York State.

What Are the Adverse Impacts?

Communities across the country have experienced a wide range of negative impacts from natural gas production.

Drinking water sources have been contaminated with explosive methane, as well as other dangerous substances, such as benzene and arsenic, that can cause cancer and other serious illnesses. Toxic chemicals, as well as erosion and runoff from drilling operations, have fouled treasured fishing streams and aquatic habitat. Leaks and spills of hazardous materials have polluted bodies of water, forests, farms, and backyards. Farmers and ranchers report serious health symptoms in livestock near natural gas operations. Exposure to open pits has killed countless birds and other wildlife. Emissions from drilling rigs, well-pad equipment, storage tanks, compressor stations, and truck traffic contribute to harmful ozone levels. The wells, roads, and pipelines that come with natural gas development can displace wildlife and fragment their habitats. And methane emissions from production sites and pipelines contribute to climate change pollution.

There have even been incidences of serious human health threats that have led families to abandon their homes in order to preserve their children's health.

Can Drilling Be Made Safer?

Yes. While virtually nothing can be made completely safe, drilling and fracking can be made safer than current operations. This is only possible if the federal and state governments act to adopt strong, enforceable laws and standards that protect the environment, public health, and communities. These must also be backed by adequate government oversight, and accompanied by corporate policies that have zero tolerance for avoidable errors. Right now, however, that is not the case.

The gas industry [should have] to adhere to critical components of the Clean Air Act, from which they are . . . currently exempt.

Cost-effective technologies exist that allow natural gas to be produced in an economical but more environmentally responsible way. For example, harmful air emissions, including methane, can be captured with the right equipment, toxic wastes can be managed in safer ways (including prohibiting their collection in open-air pits), and gas wells can be made stronger to reduce the risks of drinking water contamination from blowouts and other problems.

Some states and local governments have begun updating their rules and requiring cleaner operations. For instance, Wyoming has established better air quality protections, New Mexico has improved its waste management rules, and Colorado is working to curb stormwater runoff from fracking operations. Compared to the benefits, the costs associated with these best practices are minimal.

But while these states have taken some positive steps, they are limited and isolated examples. Most federal and state regulations have not kept up with advancements in our knowledge of the risks or with the latest technology. That is why industry can and should immediately be required to implement existing common sense, cost effective solutions to universally increase protection for human health, communities, and the environment.

New, comprehensive state and federal protections must be put in place to address, among other key safeguards, the following:

- **Reducing water pollution** by improving well construction, waste management, and monitoring of fracking operations, and requiring oil and gas corporations to comply with the sections of the Safe Drinking Water and Clean Water Acts from which they are currently exempt.

- **Reducing air pollution** by minimizing emissions that harm public health and contribute to climate change, and requiring the gas industry to adhere to critical components of the Clean Air Act, from which they are also currently exempt. Methane leak rates can and should be reduced to well below 1 percent of production.

- **Protecting communities and residential areas** by requiring industry to move fracking operations further away from homes and schools, strengthening restrictions on noise and traffic, and giving municipalities the right to use their powers to control where and how oil and gas operations occur.

- **Protecting wilderness on federal public lands,** which involves reforming policies for natural gas development on federal public lands, including new protections for wildlife habitat, air and water resources, the climate, and human health.

- **Disposing of hazardous fracking waste properly,** meaning that it should be required for all fracking waste to be subject to the hazardous waste provisions of the Resource Conservation and Recovery Act, like other hazardous waste.

- **Requiring public disclosure of chemicals** used throughout the extraction process and including the industry in the Environmental Protection Agency's (EPA) Toxics Release Inventory, which will educate communities about toxic substances on drilling sites being used in their community.

- **Developing robust scientific research on the health and environmental impacts** associated with natural gas production, and the options for preventing them.

- **Requiring air and water quality baseline testing and monitoring,** assessing the potential for exposure to harmful substances, tracking health outcomes, and including full consideration of health impacts in environmental impact studies.

- **Enhancing enforcement of the laws and safeguards,** including establishing meaningful penalties for breaking the law and creating whistleblower protections. This also includes ensuring adequate resources for regulators and inspectors, and requiring workers to report any error, accident, violation of requirements, irregular practice, or activity that otherwise jeopardizes safety and environmental protection.

Should Certain Places Be Off Limits?

Yes. Some places are simply too risky or sensitive to allow fracking to move forward, regardless of the safeguards in place.

We should not sacrifice our most important values to obtain natural gas or any other form of energy.

For instance, fracking must not take place near drinking water supplies. Adequate setbacks must be required to protect all public and private drinking water supplies. The cost and scale of an accident affecting water systems for large metropolitan areas could prove massive and irrevocable. An accident in the New York City drinking water supply alone, for example, could threaten the safe drinking water for nine million New Yorkers, as well as millions more in Philadelphia and parts of New Jersey.

States also need to ensure that adequate buffer zones are established around homes, private drinking water wells, schools, and other vulnerable community resources to protect against negative impacts of fracking, including noise, air pollution, soil contamination, surface water contamination, vibrations, and obtrusive lighting.

Additionally, part of our identity as a nation is tied to the preservation of wild lands untouched by humans, including wilderness and roadless areas. These areas provide invaluable benefits to local communities as well as tourists and visitors from around the world. Whether these irreplaceable resources exist on land, off our coasts, or deep in the ocean, they should be protected from drilling. We should not sacrifice our most important values to obtain natural gas or any other form of energy.

Americans have a right to clean water when they turn on their tap. They have a right to breathe clean air. They have a right for their voice to be heard. And they have the right to stand up when they have been wronged.

Our leaders must prioritize more efficient, cleaner, safer, and renewable sources of power that move us away from reliance on all fossil fuels. We should be sure that natural gas is being used to replace dirtier fuels, such as coal, by prioritizing renewable power sources and energy efficiency, implementing recent clean air standards, like those for mercury and sulfur, and setting strong power plant carbon pollution standards.

Strong state and federal safeguards are essential to ensure that any natural gas development occurs as safely as possible, and avoids our most sensitive lands. Where federal and state agencies are not doing enough, local governments should have the authority to protect their citizens, communities, and quality of life. NRDC opposes expanded fracking until effective safeguards are in place.

2

Hydraulic Fracturing Can Be Done Responsibly

ExxonMobil

As the country's largest natural gas producer, ExxonMobil is one of the biggest practitioners of hydraulic fracturing in the United States.

Natural gas is an abundant, affordable, and environmentally responsible energy source that is helping to meet the world's ever-growing demand for power. The natural gas extraction technique of hydraulic fracturing (fracking) helps bring this cleaner-burning energy supply to the public. Although fracking has generated a lot of recent media attention and public concern about environmental issues, it is a practice that has been safely used since the 1940s. ExxonMobil takes extensive measures to minimize the environmental impacts of fracking, supports the public disclosure of fracking chemicals and takes extra precautions to protect water supplies near its operations. Natural gas extraction creates jobs and is good for the country's energy security, so when fracking is done responsibly, everyone wins.

As the world's largest public natural gas producer, Exxon-Mobil brings supplies of this cleaner-burning energy source to global markets in a safe, reliable, and responsible manner. As part of this undertaking, we engage with stakeholders on a range of topics related to natural gas production and transportation.

Extracting natural gas from certain formations, including shale, tight sandstones, and coal beds, requires drawing the resource through openings about one half the width of a human hair. Hydraulic fracturing uses water pressure to create hairline fractures in rocks deep underground so natural gas can flow. We believe it is in everyone's interest to respond effectively to public concerns about production processes in order to maximize the benefits of this energy source. This requires industry both to properly manage associated risks, and to explain to the public and policymakers how we are doing so.

ExxonMobil's shale gas development and production activities are guided by proven policies.

All industrial processes have risks, and drilling for unconventional oil and gas is no different. We understand stakeholders are concerned about these risks, including those related to hydraulic fracturing fluids and wastewater, well casing and groundwater, vehicle traffic, air emissions, and other related effects. These are important concerns, and we know we must respond to them in every community in which we operate and reach out to communities to ensure our responses are effective.

ExxonMobil analyzes every significant operation the Corporation undertakes through our Operations Integrity Management System (OIMS). Applying OIMS requires us to identify potential safety, environmental, and social impacts and to implement procedures and processes to mitigate risks. XTO Energy Inc. (XTO), a recently acquired subsidiary of Exxon-Mobil, will fully implement OIMS, and is carrying out a risk-based, focused, and deliberate execution strategy.

ExxonMobil's shale gas development and production activities are guided by proven policies, industry guidelines and practices, as well as more than 40 years of experience in hydraulic fracturing.

We chair the American Petroleum Institute working group that has developed four recommended practice documents encompassing the life cycle of unconventional resource development. We work with state governments and multi-state entities to address concerns, establish effective regulatory frameworks, and implement industry consensus on sound management practices.

Transparency of Operations

A vital component of building community trust is transparency of operations. We support the disclosure of the ingredients used in hydraulic fracturing fluids, including on a site-specific basis. In the United States, disclosure appears on the publicly accessible FracFocus.org website, an effort between the Ground Water Protection Council and the Interstate Oil and Gas Compact Commission. Launched in April 2011, ExxonMobil and others in industry have voluntarily submitted actual data from more than 10,000 wells. In Canada, the public can access FracFocus.ca for industry disclosures in British Columbia, with Alberta and Saskatchewan planned for late 2012. We are pursuing similar disclosure approaches in Europe and other areas where we are exploring internationally. We will continue to take a leadership role in working collaboratively with communities, regulators, and industry associations to manage operational risk and address questions and concerns. ExxonMobil recognizes the importance of responsible operations in maintaining stakeholder support for this significant resource.

3

Hydraulic Fracturing Should Be Banned

Food & Water Watch

Food & Water Watch is a nonprofit consumer rights organization that focuses on corporate and government accountability relating to food, water, and fishing.

The rapid expansion of fracking in natural gas extraction has brought environmental harm to communities across the country. Accidents and leaks have polluted drinking water sources; airborne pollutants have sullied the air; and fracking wastewater bound for water treatment plants has been found to contain toxic chemicals and even radioactivity. Even if there were good regulatory oversight and strong laws governing the practice—which there are not—fracking would still pose a severe risk to public health and the environment. Instead of looking for ways to better regulate fracking, Congress should ban shale gas fracking outright, close loopholes that exempt fracking from key federal air and water regulations, and aggressively pursue renewable energy sources that would contribute to a clean-energy future.

Over the past decade, there has been a rush for new natural gas across America using a controversial—and often polluting—drilling method. Hydraulic fracturing, known as fracking, injects a mixture of water, sand and chemicals under high pressure into dense rock formations—shale, tight sandstone or coal beds—to crack the rock and release natural gas. Fracking has been around for decades, but the techniques, technologies and chemicals used to reach new, remote gas reserves are more intensive and riskier than conventional gas drilling.

Fracking wastewater contains high levels of radioactivity and other contaminants that wastewater treatment plants have had difficulty removing.

The rapid expansion of this new form of fracking has brought rampant environmental and economic problems to rural communities. Tens of billions of gallons of water are used for fracking each year, and that amount would only grow if proposed drilling moves forward. Accidents and leaks have polluted rivers, streams and drinking water supplies. Regions peppered with drilling rigs have high levels of smog as well as other airborne pollutants, including potential carcinogens. Rural communities face an onslaught of heavy truck traffic— often laden with dangerous chemicals used in drilling—and declining property values. The "bridge fuel" of fracking could well be a bridge to nowhere.

Over the past 18 months [January 2011–June 2012], at least 10 studies by scientists, Congress, investigative journalists and public interest groups have documented environmental problems with fracking. Findings include:

- Toxic chemicals present in fracking fluid could cause cancer and other health problems.

- Fracking wastewater contains high levels of radioactivity and other contaminants that wastewater treatment plants have had difficulty removing; this potentially contaminated wastewater can then be discharged into local rivers.

- In Pennsylvania, more than 3,000 gas fracking wells and permitted well sites are located within two miles of 320 day care centers, 67 schools and nine hospitals.

Fracking is exempt from key federal water protections, and federal and state regulators have allowed unchecked expansion of fracking, creating widespread environmental degradation. Overwhelmed state regulators largely oversee the practice. Even if the laws on the books were strengthened, fracking poses too severe a risk to public health and the environment to entrust effective and rigorous regulatory oversight to these officials. . . .

Ban Fracking

The lax regulation and technological advances spurred a fracking gas rush across America that some industry insiders called a "natural gas revolution" and a "game changer." Energy analysts and oil tycoon T. Boone Pickens bolstered this rush by promoting natural gas as a promising "bridge fuel" for the United States to transition from dirty fossil fuels to clean, renewable sources of energy. However, fracking itself may release enough of the greenhouse gas methane to counterbalance the lower carbon dioxide emissions from burning the natural gas. To safeguard public health and the environment, the federal government should ban shale gas fracking. . . .

The rapid expansion of horizontal hydraulic fracture drilling for natural gas has been disastrous. Federal and state regulators have been asleep at the switch as gas companies pollute the air and water of communities living in the path of the fracked gas rush. Even if the laws on the books were strengthened, fracking poses too severe a risk to public health and the environment to entrust effective and rigorous regulatory oversight to overwhelmed regulators. Both state and federal regulators have a poor track record of protecting the public from the impacts of fracking. Congress, state legislators and local governmental bodies need to ban shale gas fracking.

Rather than taking a strategic pause in the face of the demonstrable problems with fracking, President Barack Obama's administration is pursuing fracked natural gas full speed ahead.

America's fracking fad is poised to go global.

In an April 2011 speech, President Obama said that "the potential for natural gas is enormous" and promoted proposed legislation to shift from oil to natural gas—the same legislation endorsed by T. Boone Pickens to subsidize natural gas vehicles. The public opposition to fracking prompted the administration to launch a committee to figure out how to make fracking safe. This attempt is misguided—fracking is not safe.

The energy industry is spending more private money to develop controversial sources of fracked gas than the U.S. government and private sector are investing to transition to a clean energy economy. A 2011 Intergovernmental Panel on Climate Change report found that with sufficient development, renewable fuels could deliver almost 80 percent of the world's power needs by 2050. More than a bridge fuel, renewable energy is a bridge with a destination. Nonetheless, [Manchester, England's] *Guardian* reports that, "senior executives in the fossil fuel industry have launched an all-out assault on renewable energy, lobbying governments and business groups to reject wind and solar power in favor of gas."

Exporting Environmental Damage

America's fracking fad is poised to go global. China fracked its first horizontal shale gas well in April 2011 and some European countries are considering following suit. But South Africa and Quebec, Canada, have imposed fracking moratoriums, and popular opposition in France and the United Kingdom have slowed development.

Shale gas fracking poses unacceptable risks to the American public. Today, many municipalities around the country are banning fracking to protect their citizens from the negative consequences of this type of drilling. These local resolutions are a good idea, but they won't protect the entire country. Shale gas fracking should be banned on the national level. It is time to stop destroying public air and water in the interest of oil and gas company profits, and instead seek energy solutions that will provide a long term, renewable energy future for the United States.

Recommendations

- Ban shale gas fracking in the United States.

- Close loopholes that exempt fracking from key federal air and water environmental regulations.

- Aggressively invest in energy efficiency and renewable energy sources that would result in a sustainable energy future for the country.

4

Fracking Contaminates Drinking Water

Abrahm Lustgarten and Nick Kusnetz

Abrahm Lustgarten is an environmental reporter for ProPublica and a former staff writer for Fortune *magazine. He is the author of the e-book* Hydrofracked? One Man's Mystery Leads to a Backlash Against Natural Gas Drilling. *Nick Kusnetz was a 2011 Middlebury Fellow in Environmental Journalism and has covered gas drilling and energy as a reporting fellow at ProPublica. His work has appeared in* The Nation, The New York Times, *and other publications.*

In December 2011, the US Environmental Protection Agency (EPA) issued a report that for the first time scientifically linked fracking with underground water pollution. The documented contamination happened in Wyoming, where thirty-three abandoned wastewater pits leached fracking chemicals—including the cancer-causing chemicals benzene and 2-butoxyethanol—into the groundwater. The finding could be a turning point in the heated debate about whether water contamination from fracking is actually happening, as environmentalists and fracking opponents claim, or whether fracking is safe and nearby water contamination is coincidental and unrelated to the practice, as the natural gas industry maintains. The EPA is conducting a second study to determine whether fracking presents a broader risk to the country's water resources.

4

In a first, federal environment officials Thursday [December 8, 2011,] scientifically linked underground water pollution with hydraulic fracturing, concluding that contaminants found in central Wyoming were likely caused by the gas drilling process.

The findings by the Environmental Protection Agency come partway through a separate national study by the agency to determine whether fracking presents a risk to water resources.

Findings in the report . . . directly contradict longstanding arguments by the drilling industry for why the fracking process is safe.

In the 121-page draft report released Thursday, EPA officials said that the contamination near the town of Pavillion, Wyo., had most likely seeped up from gas wells and contained at least 10 compounds known to be used in frack fluids.

"The presence of synthetic compounds such as glycol ethers . . . and the assortment of other organic components is explained as the result of direct mixing of hydraulic fracturing fluids with ground water in the Pavillion gas field," the draft report states. "Alternative explanations were carefully considered."

The agency's findings could be a turning point in the heated national debate about whether contamination from fracking is happening, and are likely to shape how the country regulates and develops natural gas resources in the Marcellus Shale and across the Eastern Appalachian states.

Some of the findings in the report also directly contradict longstanding arguments by the drilling industry for why the fracking process is safe: that hydrologic pressure would naturally force fluids down, not up; that deep geologic layers provide a watertight barrier preventing the movement of chemicals towards the surface; and that the problems with the cement and steel barriers around gas wells aren't connected to fracking.

Environmental advocates greeted today's report with a sense of vindication and seized the opportunity to argue for stronger federal regulation of fracking.

"No one can accurately say that there is 'no risk where fracking is concerned,'" wrote Amy Mall, a senior policy analyst at the Natural Resources Defense Council, on her blog. "This draft report makes obvious that there are many factors at play, any one of which can go wrong. Much stronger rules are needed to ensure that well construction standards are stronger and reduce threats to drinking water."

A spokesman for EnCana, the gas company that owns the Pavillion wells, did not immediately respond to a request for comment. In an email exchange after the EPA released preliminary water test data two weeks ago, the spokesman, Doug Hock, denied that the company's actions were to blame for the pollution and suggested it was naturally caused.

"Nothing EPA presented suggests anything has changed since August of last year [2010]—the science remains inconclusive in terms of data, impact, and source," Hock wrote. "It is also important to recognize the importance of hydrology and geology with regard to the sampling results in the Pavillion Field. The field consists of gas-bearing zones in the near subsurface, poor general water quality parameters and discontinuous water-bearing zones."

Triggering a Debate

The EPA's findings immediately triggered what is sure to become a heated political debate as members of Congress consider afresh proposals to regulate fracking. After a phone call with EPA chief Lisa Jackson this morning [December 9, 2011], Sen. James Inhofe. R-Okla., told a Senate panel that he found the agency's report on the Pavillion-area contamination "offensive." Inhofe's office had challenged the EPA's investigation in Wyoming last year, accusing the agency of bias.

Residents began complaining of fouled water near Pavillion in the mid-1990s, and the problems appeared to get worse around 2004. Several residents complained that their well water turned brown shortly after gas wells were fracked nearby, and, for a time, gas companies operating in the area supplied replacement drinking water to residents.

Beginning in 2008, the EPA took water samples from resident's drinking water wells, finding hydrocarbons and traces of contaminants that seemed like they could be related to fracking. In 2010, another round of sampling confirmed the contamination, and the EPA, along with federal health officials, cautioned residents not to drink their water and to ventilate their homes when they bathed because the methane in the water could cause an explosion.

To confirm their findings, EPA investigators drilled two water monitoring wells to 1,000 feet. The agency released data from these test wells in November [2011] that confirmed high levels of carcinogenic chemicals such as benzene, and a chemical compound called 2 Butoxyethanol, which is known to be used in fracking.

Considering Multiple Causes

Still, the EPA had not drawn conclusions based on the tests and took pains to separate its groundwater investigation in Wyoming from the national controversy around hydraulic fracturing. Agriculture, drilling, and old pollution from waste pits left by the oil and gas industry were all considered possible causes of the contamination.

In the report released today [December 9, 2011], the EPA said that pollution from 33 abandoned oil and gas waste pits—which are the subject of a separate cleanup program—are indeed responsible for some degree of shallow groundwater pollution in the area. Those pits may be the source of contamination affecting at least 42 private water wells in Pavillion. But the pits could not be blamed for contamination detected in the water monitoring wells 1,000 feet underground.

That contamination, the agency concluded, had to have been caused by fracking.

Throughout its investigation in Wyoming, the EPA was hamstrung by a lack of disclosure about exactly what chemicals had been used to frack the wells.

The EPA's findings in Wyoming are specific to the region's geology; the Pavillion-area gas wells were fracked at shallower depths than many of the wells in the Marcellus shale and elsewhere.

Investigators tested the cement and casing of the gas wells and found what they described as "sporadic bonding" of the cement in areas immediately above where fracking took place. The cement barrier meant to protect the well bore and isolate the chemicals in their intended zone had been weakened and separated from the well, the EPA concluded.

The report also found that hydrologic pressure in the Pavillion area had pushed fluids from deeper geologic layers towards the surface. Those layers were not sufficient to provide a reliable barrier to contaminants moving upward, the report says.

Incomplete Information

Throughout its investigation in Wyoming, the EPA was hamstrung by a lack of disclosure about exactly what chemicals had been used to frack the wells near Pavillion. EnCana declined to give federal officials a detailed breakdown of every compound used underground. The agency relied instead on more general information supplied by the company to protect workers' health.

Hock would not say whether EnCana had used 2 BE, one of the first chemicals identified in Pavillion and known to be used in fracking, at its wells in Pavillion. But he was dismissive of its importance in the EPA's findings. "There was a single detection of 2-BE among all the samples collected in the deep monitoring wells. It was found in one sample by only one of three labs," he wrote in his reply to ProPublica two weeks ago. "Inconsistency in detection and non-repeatability shouldn't be construed as fact."

The EPA's draft report will undergo a public review and peer review process, and is expected to be finalized by spring [2012. *As of December 2012, the report had not been finalized—ed.*]

5

Fracking Pollutes the Air with Hazardous Chemicals

Jim Polson and Jim Efstathiou Jr.

Jim Polson and Jim Efstathiou Jr. are reporters for Bloomberg News, a wire service.

While most of the environmental concern about hydraulic fracturing has to do with the possibility of fracking chemicals contaminating drinking water supplies, the chemicals released into the air during the fracking process may be harmful as well. Researchers have found potentially toxic chemicals—including cancer-causing benzene—in the air near fracking sites, and they estimate a higher risk of health problems for individuals who live near those wells. New Environmental Protection Agency regulations on fracking would cut such smog-forming emissions by 25 percent and prevent the release of 3.4 tons of methane gas, which would be the equivalent of taking eleven million automobiles off the road.

Chemicals released into the air when natural gas is produced by hydraulic fracturing may pose a health risk to those living nearby, the Colorado School of Public Health said.

Researchers found potentially toxic airborne chemicals near wells in Garfield County, Colorado, during three years of monitoring, the school said today in a statement. Drilling has expanded in the county, about 180 miles (290 kilometers) west of Denver.

Emissions from the wells include methane and volatile organic compounds that react with heat and sunlight to form ozone, according to Elena Craft, a health scientist with the Environmental Defense Fund who is studying air quality near gas wells in Texas. The U.S. Environmental Protection Agency has proposed rules that would reduce oil and gas well emissions.

"If you're leaking natural gas, then you're leaking a number of pollutants including methane and volatile organic chemicals," Craft said in an interview. "Health implications? That's the million dollar question."

Hydraulic fracturing, known as fracking, has enabled oil and gas companies to access fuel trapped in previously impenetrable shale rock, reversing a decline in U.S. gas production. Environmentalists have previously raised concerns about water contamination as a result of chemicals used in fracking.

Air, Water

"It is important to include air pollution in the national dialogue on natural-gas development that has focused largely on water exposures to hydraulic fracturing," Lisa McKenzie, lead writer of the study and a research associate at the Colorado School of Public Health in Denver, said in the statement.

The research focused on those living about a half mile from the wells and was requested by county officials in response to the rapid expansion of fracking in the state. One operator has proposed drilling 200 wells about 500 feet from homes in Garfield County.

Wells near Battlement Mesa, where the research was conducted, are tapped by injecting millions of gallons of water mixed with sand and chemicals underground. The mixture is withdrawn during the process of completion as wells are readied for production.

"Non-cancer health impacts from air emissions due to natural-gas development is greater for residents living closer to wells," according to the release. "We also calculated higher cancer risks for residents living nearer to the wells."

Drillers are already reducing emissions . . . where it makes economic sense to do so.

Benzene, a carcinogen, and chemicals that can irritate eyes and cause headaches, sore throats or difficulty breathing, were found in air close to the wells. The study will be published this month in *Science of the Total Environment*, according to the statement.

The EPA proposal would cut smog-forming emissions by 25 percent through existing technologies that capture escaping gas, the agency said. The rule would also prevent the release of 3.4 million tons of methane, a greenhouse gas that's 20 times more potent than carbon dioxide. That's equal to taking 11 million passenger cars off the road, the EPA said.

According to the EPA, the rule would also lead to net gain of $30 million a year for drillers who will have more gas to market. Howard Feldman, director of regulatory and scientific affairs for the Washington-based American Petroleum Institute, said drillers are already reducing emissions from the well where it makes economic sense to do so.

"In places where people think its cost effective, they're putting in those reduced emissions controls already," Feldman said in an interview. "We think the controls may outweigh the value of the gas your capturing."

In his Jan. 24 State of the Union address, President Barack Obama said his administration would "take every possible action" to see that gas fracking is done without putting the public's health or safety at risk. A November report from a task force named by Energy Secretary Steven Chu said that among other steps to reduce the environmental impact of drillers, emissions of air pollutants, ozone precursors, and methane should be reduced "as quickly as practicable."

The EPA hasn't tried to count emissions from oil and gas wells since 1993, according to Fred Krupp, president of the Environmental Defense Fund and a member of Chu's task force. He called EPA's proposed rule "a critical step."

"Nobody has really studied the leaks from shale gas yet," Krupp said in an interview. "We all need to be searching for the data."

Texas Study

A study in Fort Worth, Texas, released in July found air pollution levels above state limits at five sites, and reported visible emissions at 296 of 388 gas well sites it examined. Fort Worth, with a population of 741,000, is in the Barnett Shale gas field and has more than 1,400 permitted wells in the city limits.

Garfield County is in Colorado's gas-producing Piceance Basin. The Colorado Department of Public Health and Environment sampled air around some gas wells in 2000, according to a 2002 report. It concluded that concentrations of non-cancer-causing chemicals in Parachute Valley, Colorado, were too low to pose significant health risk and that benzene levels were high enough to merit further study.

The Colorado Department of Public Health and Environment tested gas sites in Garfield County from 2005 to 2007, and found levels of benzene and other pollutants that were high enough to be hazardous. There weren't enough samples, though, to draw a clear conclusion, according to a white paper by the Colorado School of Public Health that urged more extensive testing.

6

Fracking Causes Seismic Instability and Earthquakes

Dusty Horwitt and Alex Formuzis

Dusty Horwitt is senior legal counsel and Alex Formuzis is vice president for media relations at the Environmental Working Group, a Washington, DC–based nonprofit whose mission is to protect public health and the environment through research and advocacy in the areas of toxic chemicals, agricultural subsidies, public lands, and corporate accountability.

The US Geological Service has linked natural gas extraction to seismic instability and small earthquakes in regions where natural gas drilling is taking place. Researchers found that as the rate of drilling and the use of hydraulic fracturing fluids increased in an area, so did the frequency of earthquakes—sometimes dramatically. Researchers believe that the increase in the number of wells drilled, the widespread use of hydraulic fracturing, and the disposal of used fracking fluids by injecting them into waste wells are all contributing factors. An Environmental Protection Agency task force is working on guidelines for "managing or minimizing" earthquakes caused by underground injection wells that hold fracking wastewater. Such recommendations will be especially important in California, where natural gas fracking takes place near known major fault lines.

A U.S. Geological Survey research team has linked oil and natural gas drilling operations to a series of recent earthquakes from Alabama to the Northern Rockies.

According to the study led by USGS geophysicist William Ellsworth, the spike in earthquakes since 2001 near oil and gas extraction operations is "almost certainly man-made." The research team cites underground injection of drilling wastewater as a possible cause.

"With gasoline prices at $4 a gallon, there's pressure to rush ahead with drilling, but the USGS report is another piece of evidence that shows we have to proceed carefully," said Dusty Horwitt, Senior Counsel and chief natural resources analyst at Environmental Working Group [EWG]. "We can't afford multi-million-dollar water pollution cleanups or earthquakes that could pose risks to homes and health."

A possible explanation [for more earthquakes] is the increase in the number of wells drilled over the past decade and the increase in fluid used in the hydraulic fracturing of each well.

The USGS study, published by the Seismological Society of America, will be presented at the group's meeting April 17–19 [2012] in San Diego, CA.

The authors shared their findings with *EnergyWire*'s Mike Soraghan in an article published March 29 [2012]. Soraghan wrote:

The study found that the frequency of earthquakes started rising in 2001 across a broad swath of the country between Alabama and Montana. In 2009, there were 50 earthquakes greater than magnitude-3.0, the abstract states, then 87 quakes in 2010. The 134 earthquakes in the zone last year is a sixfold increase over 20th century levels.

The USGS authors said they do not know why oil and gas activity might cause an increase in earthquakes but a possible explanation is the increase in the number of wells drilled over the past decade and the increase in fluid used in the hydraulic fracturing of each well. The combination of factors is likely creating far larger amounts of wastewater that companies often inject into underground disposal wells. Scientists have linked these disposal wells to earthquakes since as early as the 1960s. The injections can induce seismicity by changing pressure and adding lubrication along faults.

More Wells Means More Waste

The U.S. Energy Information Administration reports that between 1991 and 2000, oil and gas companies drilled 245,000 wells in the U.S. compared to 405,000 wells between 2001 and 2010—a 65 percent increase. As an example of how much more fracking fluid is used, New York state's review of oil and natural gas drilling regulations in 1988 assumed that companies would use between 20,000 and 80,000 gallons of fluid for hydraulic fracturing per well. The state's 2011 review of regulations for natural gas drilling in shale formations assumed that companies would use 2.4 million to 7.8 million gallons of fluid per well—a 100-fold increase.

According to Anthony Ingraffea, a professor of engineering at Cornell University who has conducted research on hydraulic fracturing, the increase in both the number of wells drilled and the amount of hydraulic fracturing fluid used per well has been driven by a shift of drilling into so-called unconventional formations such as shale in which gas and oil are distributed over very large volumes of rock, which need stimulation by fracking. Companies have increasingly tapped these formations because they have depleted most of the conventional formations in which gas and oil are contained in a relatively concentrated pool. In these conventional formations, companies can simply perforate the pool with their drill bit and drain a significant quantity of oil or gas. In unconventional formations, however, energy companies must drill more wells because the energy deposits are widely dispersed. Drillers must also use significantly more fracturing fluid to create larger fractures that can access a broader area of oil or gas.

"The rate of drilling and the volume of fluid used have increased tremendously," said Ingraffea.

The USGS report is likely to be of particular interest in California where earthquakes are a part of life largely as a result of the 810-mile-long San Andreas Fault.

The Environmental Protection Agency [EPA] regulates underground waste disposal wells under its underground injection control program. The agency often delegates primary enforcement authority to the states. According to an article written by Soraghan and published in the March 15, 2012 edition of *EnergyWire*, an EPA task force is preparing recommendations for "managing or minimizing" earthquakes caused by underground injection wells. "The group appears to have receded from its initial goal of finding ways to 'avoid' earthquakes caused by injection," Soraghan reported. An EPA presentation included in the article showed that the EPA sets specific standards for avoiding earthquakes for some types of injection wells but in the case of oil and gas wastewater injection wells, such measures are up to the agency's discretion.

The USGS report is likely to be of particular interest in California where earthquakes are a part of life largely as a result of the 810-mile-long San Andreas Fault. An EWG investigation recently discovered that companies are engaged in hydraulic fracturing, mostly for oil, in a number of counties throughout California, including several directly above the fault line. It is unclear how the companies are disposing of their wastewater.

7

The Truth About Fracking

Kevin D. Williamson

Kevin D. Williamson is deputy managing editor of National Review *magazine.*

Natural gas extraction operations are being run by a new breed of young engineers who are dedicated to solving the industry's technical and environmental challenges. There are some valid concerns about fracking—such as wastewater disposal and noise—but they are not insurmountable and have been unnecessarily hyped in the media. While methane migration can indeed cause tapwater to become flammable, fracking itself is not responsible for it. Similarly, it would be impossible for fracking wastewater to contaminate aquifers because the wells are so deep and there is so much solid rock between the wells and water sources. Opponents of fracking and natural gas extraction in general have greatly exaggerated the dangers, which are all quite manageable. Science supports the safety of fracking.

In the middle-of-frackin'-nowhere Pennsylvania, Boy Genius is showing off his giant robot: It's about 150 feet tall, God and the almighty engineers alone know how many hundreds of tons of steel, and four big, flat duck feet on bright orange legs. "Yeah, this is kind of cool," he says of his supersized Erector Set project. "You can set those feet at 45 degrees, and it will walk around in circles all day," a colleague adds.

But Boy Genius is not letting himself get too excited about all this—it's pretty clearly not his first giant robot, and he's a lot more excited about his seismic-imaging system: "It's kind of like a GPS, but it's underground and it works with the Earth's magnetic characteristics." Nods all around—that is cool. Everybody here has a three-day beard and a hardhat and steel-toed work boots, but there's a strong whiff of chess club and Science Olympiad in the air, young men who are no strangers to the pocket protector, who in adolescence discovered an unusual facility for fluid dynamics and now are beavering away at mind-clutchingly complex technical problems, one of which is how to get a 150-foot-tall tower of machinery from A to B without taking it apart and trucking it (solution: add feet). That giant robot may walk, but it isn't too fast: It can take half a day to move 20 feet, because this isn't a Transformers movie, this is The Play, and Boy Genius is a member of the startlingly youthful and bespectacled tribe of engineers swarming out of the University of Pittsburgh and the Colorado School of Mines and Penn State and into the booming gas fields of Pennsylvania, where the math weenies are running the show in the Marcellus shale, figuring out how to relentlessly suck a Saudi Arabia's worth of natural gas out of a vein of hot and impermeable rock thousands of feet beneath the green valleys of Penn's woods. Forget about your wildcatters, your roughnecks, your swaggering Texans in big hats: The nerds have taken over.

Tens of thousands of new jobs have already been created, . . . and tens of billions of dollars in new wealth has been injected into the ailing U.S. economy, since Marcellus production really picked up around 2008.

The weird little in-house argot of gas exploration has more plays than Stephen Sondheim: the conventional gas play, the shallow gas play, the Gothic play, the Wyoming play, and the gold-plated godfather of them all, the Marcellus play, which stretches from West Virginia to New York and contains hundreds of trillions of cubic feet of natural gas. Exactly how much recoverable gas is down there is a matter of hot dispute, but the general consensus is: a whole bunch, staggering amounts quantified in numbers that have to be written in exponential expressions (maybe it's 1.7×10^{14} cubic feet, maybe 4.359×10^{14}), with the estimates on the higher end suggesting the equivalent of 15 years of total U.S. energy use. There's so much efficiently combustible stuff down there that the boy geniuses have to spend hours in esoteric preparations for what to do about the oil and gas they hit that they don't mean to— they're after the Marcellus gas, but there's a lot of other methane on the way down.

Given that oil imports account for about half of the total U.S. trade deficit, that U.S. policymakers suffer from debilitating insomnia every time some random ayatollah starts making scary noises about the Strait of Hormuz, and that about half of American electricity comes from burning coal—which, on its very best day, is a lot more environmentally problematic than natural gas (something to think about while tooling down to Trader Joe's in your 45-percent coal-powered Chevy Volt or Nissan Leaf)—exploiting natural gas to its full capability has the potential to radically alter some fundamental economic, national-security, and environmental equations of keen interest in these overextended and underemployed United States. Tens of thousands of new jobs already have been created (want $60,000 a year to drive a water truck with a $2,000 signing bonus? Pennsylvania is calling), and tens of billions of dollars in new wealth has been injected into the ailing U.S. economy, since Marcellus production really picked up around 2008. Pennsylvania and West Virginia saw 57,000 new Marcellus jobs in a single year, as firms ranging from scrappy independents to giants such as Royal Dutch Shell poured billions of dollars into shale investments—land, equipment, buildings, roads, machinery: capital, in a word. Massive capital.

Cheap, relatively clean, ayatollah-free energy, enormous investments in real capital and infrastructure, thousands of new jobs for blue-collar workers and Ph.D.s alike, Americans engineering something other than financial derivatives—who could not love all that?

Josh, mostly.

Everybody in the Marcellus play is on a first-name basis with Josh Fox, even though few of them have met the young director who with a single fraudulent image in his documentary *Gasland*—footage of a Colorado man turning on his kitchen sink and setting the tap water on fire—brought into existence a new crusade for the Occupy Whatever set and a new Public Enemy No. 1 for the Luddite Left: gas exploration, specifically the extraction technique of hydraulic fracturing, popularly known as "fracking."

Fracking works like this: You set up your giant robot and you drill a five-inch-diameter hole down several thousand feet until you hit the gas shale, and then you turn 90 degrees and you drill horizontally through some more shale, until you've got all your pipes and rig in place. And then you hit that shale with a high-pressure blast of water and sand, creating millimeter-wide fractures through which the natural gas can escape and make you very, very rich in spite of the fact that you're spending about a million dollars a week on space-age "matrix" drill bits and squadrons of engineers and a small army of laborers, technicians, truck drivers, machinists, and a pretty-good-sized bill from Hoggfather's, the local barbecue joint that has added a couple of specialized and custom-outfitted mobile crews just for cooking two massive meals a day for the fracking hands who are far too busy to take off for lunch. (Sure, ExxonMobil is going to be making a killing, but fracking's biggest boosters may be the local restaurateurs who are cooking with gas while cooking for gas, and are happy to serve workers straight from the field: "No Mud on the Floor, No Cash in the Drawer" says the sign in a local diner.) The water makes the fractures, and the sand keeps them open. There's some other stuff in that fracking blend, too: biocides, for one thing, not very different from what's in your swimming pool, to keep bacteria and algae and other gunk from growing in the water and clogging up the works. There are also some friction reducers, because water and sand moving at speed can produce a lot of wear and tear (cf. the Grand Canyon), and the occasional jolt of 7 percent hydrochloric acid solution for boring out holes in the concrete. The mix is 99+ percent water and sand, and the rest of the stuff is mostly run-of-the-mill industrial chemicals (those friction-reducers use a polymer that also is used in children's toys, for example). Real concerns, but not exactly an insurmountable environmental challenge.

The weird true thing is that water has been catching fire for a long time—"long time" here meaning way back into the mists of obscure prehistory.

Not only is this happening more than a mile beneath the surface, it's also happening at a level that is separated from the closest points of the aquifer by a layer of impermeable rock three or four or five Empire State Buildings deep. "We couldn't frack through that if we were *trying* to," says one engineer working the Marcellus. "The idea that we could do so by accident is crazy. Not while we're fracking with water and sand. Nukes, maybe, but not water and sand."

So what about that burning water?

The weird true thing is that water has been catching fire for a long time—"long time" here meaning way back into the mists of obscure prehistory and the realm of legend. The temple of the Oracle of Delphi was built on the site of a burning spring said to have been discovered by a bewildered goatherd around 1000 B.C., and sundry antique heathens across the Near East had rituals related to burning bodies of water. The geographically minded among you will appreciate that there are several places in the United States named "Burning Springs," including prominent ones in such energy-intensive locales as Kentucky and West Virginia. There's a Burning Springs in New York, too, and 17th-century missionaries wrote in awe about Indians' setting fire to the waters of Lake Erie and nearby streams. Water wells were catching fire in Pennsylvania as early as the 18th century, well before anybody was fracking for gas.

You wouldn't know it from watching *Gasland*, but that Colorado community made famous by the film has had water catching on fire since at least the 1930s, and the Colorado division of water chronicled "troublesome amounts of . . . methane" in the water back in 1976. As it turns out, places that have a lot of gas in the ground *have a lot of gas in the ground*. And sometimes that gas is in the water, too, as the result of natural geological processes.

The problem with fracking mostly isn't what goes down the pipe, but what comes up.

Which isn't to say that gas drilling can't muck up drinking-water wells. That can and does happen—but it has nothing to do with fracking. If anything, fracking is less likely to pollute groundwater than are other forms of drilling, because it happens so far from the water, with so much rock in between, which isn't the case with shallower wells and more traditional forms of gas exploration.

"Methane migration is real," says John Hanger, an environmental activist in Pennsylvania who served as head of the state's department of environmental protection under the liberal governorship of Democrat Ed Rendell. "Prior to the Marcellus, there have probably been 50 to 150 private water wells, out of more than a million in the state, that have had methane contamination as a result of mistakes in the drilling process—but that has nothing to do with fracking. Some in the industry deny that it ever happens, and that is false. But frack fluids returning from depth, from 5,000 to 8,000 feet under the ground, to contaminate an aquifer? When the industry says that's never happened, that has in fact *never happened.*"

Colorado's gas regulator took the unusual step of releasing a public debunking of *Gasland*'s claim that fracking is responsible for that flaming faucet. Confronted with the facts—call them "an inconvenient truth"—Fox responded that they were "not relevant." But what is not relevant is that image of a burning water faucet, at least if you want to understand the facts about fracking, which the anti-frack fanatics don't.

Disposing of wastewater is a challenge from all sides: PR, economic, technical, environmental, and economic.

The problem with fracking mostly isn't what goes down the pipe, but what comes up, and the real hairy environmental challenge turns out to be the relatively un-sexy matter of wastewater management. Gas drillers put their bits down through a lot of ancient seabeds, meaning that the water comes up saturated with our tasty friend NaCl, a.k.a. salt. Given that a great many examples of aquatic and riparian flora and fauna are evolved to do well in fresh water but curl up and die in salt water—especially salt water that's considerably saltier than the saltiest seawater—you can't just dump that stuff in the Susquehanna River. And then there's potassium salts and such. And then there's other stuff that comes up, too, substances you'd just as soon see remain buried in the depths of the earth: arsenic, for one thing, and the darkly whispered-about entity known in drilling circles as NORM—Naturally Occurring Radioactive Material—and various other kinds of Very Bad Stuff. Of particular concern is the presence of bromides, which, when combined with the chlorine used in water-treatment facilities, have a worrisome tendency to turn into the SEAL TEAM SIX of volatile organic compounds, basically a big flashing neon sign reading "CANCER."

There are other workaday environmental problems endemic to fracking: For the three to five days a frack lasts, it's loud—really, really loud, because it's basically a construction site, with a vast array of pumps and compressors and giant margarita mixers blending sand into the water, and a big battery of generators to run it all. There's not much to be done about the noise, though you're typically not fracking real close to densely populated areas. A few firms have hit upon the novel approach of simply offering nearby homeowners money to go away for the week, expenses paid, or at least putting them up in a hotel for the duration. (An idled fracking rig might cost you $1 million a week—you can afford to pay a lot of HoJo bills to keep that from happening.) The trucks cause traffic snarls, so they're building more pipelines to replace the trucks, but digging pipelines can be an inconvenience, too. Fracking for gas is not zero-impact. There's no easy way around that.

And there's certainly no easy way around the water issues, either. Disposing of wastewater is a challenge from all sides: PR, economic, technical, environmental, and economic. But a number of the drillers have come up with a nearly ideal solution for disposing of it: Don't.

A couple of hundred miles away from Boy Genius and his giant robot, in the Marcellus heartland of Williamsport, Pa., is TerrAqua Resource Management, one of the many private firms that have sprung up throughout THE PLAY to do what the local wastewater-treatment plants and municipal authorities aren't equipped to do and probably shouldn't be expected to do: treat nasty drilling water so that it can be used again. Trucks pull up, unload their murky liquid cargo, and then fill up on usable water to take back to the next job. Inside, a trio of vast water tanks, chemical vats, some sand filters, and a bunch more engineers make that water reusable. The facility has been up and running for only a couple of years, but millions of gallons of water already have passed through it. The solids get filtered out and disposed of, bacteria get biocided, and everybody makes the department of environmental protection happy by providing a government-certified "beneficial reuse" of drilling water.

Recycling water rather than discharging it has been a fundamental change for the industry's environmental impact.

Interesting thing: The place doesn't stink. It's got a slightly earthy smell to it, like the nursery section at Home Depot, but it doesn't smell like you'd expect a water-treatment plant to smell. TerrAqua makes its living from the dirty end of the gas business, and its executives are under no illusions about the industry. There are good eggs—or at least self-interested, large-cap eggs who appreciate how much they have to lose if they get sloppy—and then there are what the locals call the "gassholes," by which they do not mean to denote the channel down which the pipe goes.

"There's *compliance*, and there's *high* compliance," says TerrAqua vice president Marty Muggleton. "There are companies that like to have a lot of extra cushion between where they are and where they have to be, and then there are those who like to get their toes close to the edge. And I think the industry has figured out which one of those you really want to be."

The one you want to be, everybody from environmental activists to industry insiders says, is a company like Range Resources, a Texas-based firm that owns a big part of THE PLAY south of Pittsburgh, operating out of the hamlet of Canonsburg, Pa., near the West Virginia border. Like practically everybody else in town, they have a bunch of shiny new space in a corporate park that was barely half-populated until the Marcellus began to get going. It's a busy anthill with a lot of boots and surprisingly few suits. Range is one of the companies that have figured out that there's so much money coming out of the shale—even with gas down near $2—that it pays to go above and beyond. Their trucks tear up the roads in Canonsburg, so they build newer and better roads than the ones they found, spending more money on roads than the city itself does. There are a surprising number of speed traps around town, but they aren't the local Barney Fifes: They're contractors hired by Range, keeping an eye on the company's drivers, who get fired for speeding or otherwise behaving in a gassholish fashion. The old days of what they call "Texas-style" gas development are mostly in the past: The billion-dollar boys have a lot of resources to throw at environmental problems and a lot to lose.

"Pennsylvania used to have surface disposal," says Range's Matt Pitzarella, "and West Virginia still does. That's just crazy." "Surface disposal" means "just dumping it in the river or on the ground." Pennsylvania, he points out, has a long history of environmental grief related to the energy industry, from acidic mine discharges to thousands of forgotten (and not always well-capped) oil wells dating from back in the days of Colonel Drake, the genius who noticed that farmers drilling water wells kept hitting oil and figured he might as well drill for the oil. Thousands of steel casings were ripped out of wells during World War II, and thousands of miles of waterways in the state have been befouled, mostly by mine discharges. Natural gas is pretty clean at the combustion point, and Range wants to be the firm that shows how clean it can be during the preceding stages. "If anything, the microscope that we as an industry are under has made us more innovative. Some of the tactics they use may be unfair. It's not fair to paint us all with the same broad brush. But at the same time, it's not fair for the industry to paint all the environmentalists with the same broad brush, either." Recycling water rather than discharging it has been a fundamental change for the industry's environmental impact and, as long as the water is cleaned up enough that it doesn't muck up the works, it's all the same to the drillers. "We could frack with peanut butter, if we had enough of it," Pitzarella says.

Keeping regulation at the state level is the top political priority in the Marcellus.

Fracking with Skippy never occurred to George Mitchell, the legendary gasman who staked his fortune on the seemingly crackpot idea that you could efficiently get gas out of a rock, but he tried everything else. Range engineer Mark Whitley was with Mitchell in the early days, and still gets a little edge in his voice when he talks about the dicey prospect of having invested about $1 billion of a company worth only about that much in a technology that nobody thought would work. Noting that President Obama claimed that "it was public research dollars" that made shale extraction possible, he laughs without mirth, and looks like he wants to spit: "Not true," he says. "We tried everything known to man to get a rock to produce. There's a lot of people who claim to be the father of the Marcellus, but if you didn't put any money in or take any gas out, then what's that? It was industry studies, industry experience, and industry dollars that did this, and we've driven up production more rapidly than anybody thought possible." And it was far from a done deal for years: "We could have thrown in the towel any time during the first ten years, but the one guy who didn't want to quit was the guy in charge: George." (George. Not, incidentally, Barack.) They tried all sorts of brews to get the shale to give up the gas, and, as the expenses mounted, they tried cheaper and cheaper alternatives, eventually settling on the low-tech combination of water and sand that turned out to be the thing that actually works. "Economics drove it," Whitley says.

The gas guys scoff at President Obama's claim that federal ingenuity produced the shale boom, and they scoff harder at their rivals' occasional pleas for government handouts, notably T. Boone Pickens's plan to have the government require long-haul trucks to convert to natural gas and then have taxpayers pick up the bill for it. "The best thing the federal government can do is stay out of our way," Whitley says. "Leave us alone, and we are happy. We are well and appropriately regulated by the state."

Practically everybody in the industry speaks well, if sometimes begrudgingly, of Pennsylvania's department of environmental protection, which, after being caught flat-footed in the early days of the shale revolution, has gotten with the program in a big way. It's undergone a major overhaul of its regulatory regime, and by most measures Pennsylvania's gas industry is cleaner and safer today than in the pre-fracking era. Billions of dollars rolling in, and thousands of new jobs, and much more on the line in the future, will do that. And the industry, while not always entirely in love with the DEP and its colonoscopic minions, appreciates that its Pennsylvania regulators understand the practices and geology of Pennsylvania in a way that faraway regulators at the EPA would not. If the EPA—especially Barack Obama's highly politicized EPA—gets involved, the result is likely to be arbitrary national standards. "The feds only screw things up," says one engineer, and any reasonable federal regulatory regime would end up essentially replicating most or all of what the states already are doing, but at a political distance that makes regulators more remote and less accountable. When it comes to fracking for gas, facts on the ground are facts literally in the ground. Keeping regulation at the state level is the top political priority in the Marcellus, so the industry has an interest in making the DEP look good: It's that compliance-vs.-high compliance thing again, naked self-interest producing virtuous outcomes. Range regularly has the DEP out to its facilities to show them the latest and greatest, with the unspoken suggestion that what it does voluntarily everybody else in THE PLAY should do voluntarily, too, because voluntarily accepted best practices are the only real political insurance against involuntarily accepted second-best (or worse) practices: Let's do it right before the feds make us do it wrong.

DEP spokesman Kevin Sunday encourages that line of thinking: "Pennsylvania has a unique and diverse geology, and that's why states should have the primacy in regulating this instead of the one-size-fits-all approach that some in the federal government would prefer to see." He says that water recycling has represented a "sea change" in the industry. "Some are recycling at 100 percent—it depends on what you're drilling through. The average is 70, 75 percent." Higher standards for discharged water have made it more attractive to recycle, too, with many facilities required to treat water to the state's standard for potable drinking water before putting it into streams or rivers. That's a sneaky little trick: Once the water has been cleaned up enough to discharge, nobody wants to discharge it. "If you get it down to that standard, it's too valuable to flush it down the toilet," Sunday says.

Which is to say that in the Marcellus they have discovered, along with enormous quantities of gas, that rarest of commodities: a regulatory success story.

"There is no doubt that drilling wastewater is highly polluted," says Hanger, the former DEP secretary. "Prior to the Marcellus, when the Pennsylvania industry was small, we were dumping drilling wastewater untreated into rivers and streams and hoping that dilution would keep concentrations below levels that would cause damage to aquatic life or drinking water. There is probably less water going untreated into the rivers today than before the first Marcellus well. It's a success story. If you look at the top ten things impacting water in

Pennsylvania right now, the gas industry would not be on the list, and certainly not fracking. Industry, environmentalists, and regulators all ought to be celebrating. But there's money to be made out of fighting."

Consumers and policymakers should understand the limitations of [alternative] technologies.

All of which is perplexing to the boy geniuses in the fracking command centers scattered around Pennsylvania. Talking politics with engineers is dancing about architecture—they just don't get it, and they get frustrated. "We have all this wealth in the ground," says one of the bespectacled brethren, "and we can get it out. We can do it efficiently and cleanly"—and we have giant frackin' robots!—"but some people don't want us to. They just don't like it." Laying out this scenario, he wears a look that is four parts nonplussed and one part hurt. You want to hand the kid an Ayn Rand novel with the good parts dog-eared.

Nothing happens in a vacuum, political or environmental, even a mile under the rock. And the real question about fracking, as Hanger points out, isn't fracking vs. some Platonic energy ideal. It's between fracking and coal, or, to a lesser extent, between fracking and oil.

Walking around finished gas wells in THE PLAY, you'll notice a weird thing: A lot of them run off of solar power. There's no utility power in some of the more remote areas, and it's more efficient to put up some solar panels to run the monitoring equipment and the other gear necessary to keep a producing well producing. And in the remote Texas panhandle, Valero operates a major oil refinery that's attached to a 5,000-acre wind farm, being located in the sweet spot of having lots of crude pipelines, lots of wind, lots of real estate, and not very many people. When it's operating at its peak, the wind farm produces enough juice to run the whole refinery—but it takes a lot of turbines and a lot of West Texas wind to get that done when you have the capacity to refine 170,000 barrels of crude a day. The wind farm isn't a PR stunt, Valero insists: It's economical, and beyond wind Valero has a pretty good-sized portfolio of investments in alternative energy, from ethanol to algae. But consumers and policymakers should understand the limitations of those technologies, a Valero spokesman says: "We get frustrated by this idea that cars should run on sunshine and happy thoughts." But cars can and do run on natural gas, and the surge in U.S. oil and gas production has made American firms more competitive with their overseas rivals and has led to a renaissance among local refineries.

Given all that, the data are on the side of fracking. But the political momentum is on the other side. It remains likely that the EPA will take its heavy hand to the industry, a development for which the enviro-Left, led by Occupy Wall Street, is positively howling, which is frustrating for environmentalists such as John Hanger. "If there's no fracking, the unavoidable consequence would be a sharp increase in oil and coal consumption. Even if environmental and public-health issues were your only concerns—leave aside national security and the economic impacts—that fact alone should give you some pause."

But don't bother with *evidence*: The opposition to fracking isn't at its heart environmental or economic or scientific.

It's ideological, and that ideology is nihilism. Environmentalism is a movement that began with the fire on the Cuyahoga River in 1969 and a few brief years later had mutated into the Voluntary Human Extinction Movement (motto: "May we live long and die out!"), which maintains: "Phasing out the human race by voluntarily ceasing to breed will allow Earth's biosphere to return to good health. Crowded conditions and resource shortages will improve as we become less dense." (Good luck with that "less dense" thing, geniuses.)

Benign environmentalists are opposed to pollution, as all sensible people are; malign environmentalists are opposed to energy and most of what it enables. Their enemy isn't drilling rigs and ethane crackers and engineers and their technological marvels: Their enemy is the kind of civilization that makes such feats and wonders possible, the fact that a smart guy with a big idea can make a hole in the ground and summon up power from the vasty deep. Their enemy is *us*. We can debate best drilling practices, appropriate emissions regulation, wastewater-disposal techniques—the engineering stuff—and even hare-brained ideas like the Pickens plan.

But we can't really debate the course of modern technological civilization with people who are opposed to modern technological civilization per se, your mostly middle-class and expensively miseducated (and forgive me for noticing but your overwhelmingly white) types afflicted with the ennui of affluence, who suddenly take a fancy to the idea that life might be lived more authentically with a bone in one's nose and a trip to the neighborhood shaman—the shaman who might, if the spirits smile upon him, initiate you into the ancient mysteries of the burning spring.

8

Americans Favor Stricter Regulations for Fracking

Jim Efstathiou Jr.

Jim Efstathiou Jr. is a reporter for Bloomberg News, a wire service.

Most Americans believe that there should be stronger regulations to govern the practice of hydraulic fracturing. In a national poll conducted by Bloomberg News in 2012, more than three times as many people said that more regulations were needed as opposed to fewer regulations. Those findings complement those from other surveys in New York and Ohio in which most of the people questioned said they believe that fracking causes environmental damage. New York has now halted natural gas drilling until new regulations are enacted to protect water sources and provide better oversight for fracking. The US Environmental Protection Agency continues its own research on the impacts of fracking and is in the process of putting together new federal regulations to govern natural gas extraction practices.

The U.S. public favors greater regulation of hydraulic fracturing, a natural gas drilling technique that has reduced prices for consumers while raising environmental concerns.

More than three times as many Americans say there should be more regulation of fracturing, known as fracking, than less, according to a Bloomberg News National Poll conducted March 8–11. The findings coincide with recent surveys in

Ohio and New York where people who believe fracking will cause environmental damage outnumber those who say the process is safe.

"That actually doesn't surprise me," Mark Boling, executive vice president for Houston-based Southwestern Energy Co. (SWN), said of the poll results in an interview. "We have been so focused as an industry on figuring out how to crack the code and get these huge volumes of gas trapped in shale formations. We haven't focused on the things we have to do differently above ground."

When asked ... if there needs to be more or less regulation of fracking, 65 percent [of surveyed persons] said more, 18 percent said less and 17 percent said they weren't sure.

Because of fracking, the U.S. is producing so much gas that the government may approve an export terminal after warning four years ago of a need to boost imports. Gas from shale, fine-grained sedimentary rocks that trap the fuel, made up 23 percent of U.S. production in 2010, and is forecast to rise to 49 percent by 2035, according to the Energy Department.

Fracking Jobs

In 2010, the industry supported more than 600,000 U.S. jobs, according to a report that consultants IHS Global Insight prepared for America's Natural Gas Alliance, a group that represents drillers. Gas prices fell 36 percent last year, helping to put U.S. household expenditures for gas this winter on a track to be the lowest in nine years.

When asked by Bloomberg if there needs to be more or less regulation of fracking, 65 percent said more, 18 percent said less and 17 percent said they weren't sure. The poll of 1,002 adults 18 and older was conducted by Selzer & Co., a

Des Moines, Iowa–based firm. It has a margin of error of plus or minus 3.1 percentage points.

In fracking, millions of gallons of chemically treated water and sand are forced underground to break up rock and allow gas or oil to flow. Environmental groups have raised concerns over harmful emissions and the handling of wastewater from gas wells.

State Regulation

Fracking has been used in places such as Texas and Oklahoma since 1949 and is largely regulated by the states. Its use has expanded with the adoption of horizontal wells that branch off to tap into more gas from a single well.

In Pennsylvania, Ohio and West Virginia, drillers are tapping a formation known as the Marcellus Shale that may hold enough gas to supply the U.S. for six years.

The drilling boom has also produced some high-profile failures that have prompted state regulators to review standards. In Pennsylvania, rules were beefed up after the state found that gas from wells operated by Chesapeake Energy Corp. (CHK) had seeped into drinking water supplies in 2010. In his Jan. 24 State of the Union address, President Barack Obama said his administration would "take every possible action" to see that gas fracking is done without putting the public's health or safety at risk. The U.S. Environmental Protection Agency is investigating claims that the extraction process tainted drinking water in Wyoming and Pennsylvania.

New York Moratorium

Former New York Governor David Paterson put a moratorium on drilling while regulators draft rules to protect water sources such as the unfiltered watershed that provides 1.3 billion gallons (4.9 billion liters) a day to New York City.

Proposed regulations threaten to slow shale-gas development and the growth of new jobs, according to the American

Petroleum Institute, which represents oil and gas companies. Kyle Isakower, vice president for regulatory and economic policy for the Washington-based industry group, warned of a wave of new federal regulations.

"We're concerned that there are now 10 separate federal government agencies looking to study and potentially add new and unnecessary layers of regulations on hydraulic fracturing," Isakower said in a March 1 statement. "More regulation could increase costs and delays for operators."

> *The [Environmental Protection Agency has] linked fracking to groundwater contamination.*

The EPA has proposed rules that would reduce emissions from gas wells and set standards for how to treat wastewater. The agency is also conducting a broad study on the potential impacts of gas fracking on drinking water. Preliminary results are scheduled to be released later this year.

"I don't see it as something where the federal government is moving into an area where they haven't traditionally had jurisdiction," Boling said. "I don't see a problem with that."

Boling is part of an industry group working on a project with the New York–based Environmental Defense Fund to help states improve oversight of gas fracking.

In December, the EPA linked fracking to groundwater contamination in Pavillion, Wyoming. The agency is also testing water from wells in Dimock, Pennsylvania, after residents in the community complained of methane and chemical contamination from wells operated by Cabot Oil & Gas Corp. (COG)

That inquiry prompted Cabot Chief Executive Officer Dan Dinges to say the "EPA's actions in Dimock appear to undercut the president's stated commitment to this important resource," according to a Jan. 26 letter to EPA Administrator Lisa Jackson. "EPA's approach has caused confusion that undermines important policy goals of the United States to ensure safe, reliable, secure and clean energy sources from domestic natural gas."

Still, Pennsylvania residents strongly support shale gas production. When asked if drilling should go forward in light of its economic benefits or stop because of potential environmental impacts, 62 percent chose drilling compared with 30 percent who said there should be no drilling, according to a survey by Quinnipiac University in Hamden, Connecticut. The poll of 1,370 registered voters was conducted Sept. 21–26.

People in New York and Ohio expressed greater concern over environmental damage, according to Quinnipiac. In a January survey of 1,610 registered voters in Ohio, 43 percent said fracking would cause environmental damage and 16 percent said it would not. When asked the same question in December, 55 percent of people surveyed in New York said drilling would damage the environment while 13 percent said it would not.

9

States Are the Proper Regulators of Natural Gas Drilling

Michael L. Krancer

Michael L. Krancer is secretary of the Department of Environmental Protection for the Commonwealth of Pennsylvania.

As natural gas extraction operations have expanded and taken on greater importance as an energy source, it has prompted some people to call for closer scrutiny and more regulation of the industry by the federal government. This is unnecessary, however; individual states are already doing a good job of regulating fracking by means of their existing laws. State laws that govern air and water quality, solid waste management, drilling practices and environmental protection are perfectly adequate to regulate natural gas extraction operations, including fracking, if they are properly enforced. There is no evidence that new federal statutes are needed to regulate fracking. The FRAC Act would be an unnecessary layer of bureaucracy that could hinder the ability of the natural gas industry to create jobs and generate economic growth.

[Editor's note: The Fracturing Responsibility and Awareness of Chemicals (FRAC) Act was originally introduced to both houses of Congress in June 2009 and was reintroduced in

March 2011. The bill would amend the Safe Drinking Water Act to repeal the exemption from restrictions on underground injection of fluids near drinking water sources granted to hydraulic fracturing operations and would also require the disclosure of fracking chemicals. As of December 2012, the FRAC Act was still in committee and had not been brought to the floor of either house of Congress.]

The potential of the Marcellus Shale play has captured the world's attention. Indeed, not since Edwin Drake drilled North America's first commercial oil well in 1859 have so many focused their attention on Pennsylvania as an opportunity for oil and gas development. Increased well drilling has also brought with it unfounded skepticism about Pennsylvania's ability to properly oversee the oil and gas industry.

Pennsylvania Regulation

I say unfounded because just last year [2010] the head of EPA's [Environmental Protection Agency's] Drinking Water Program said publicly that "I have no information that states aren't doing a good job already [regulating fracking]." That is certainly the case for Pennsylvania. Also, our regulatory program was recently evaluated by the independent, non-profit, multi-stakeholder State Review of Oil and Natural Gas Environmental Regulations organization (STRONGER) and received positive marks. STRONGER was only recently recognized by the United States Department of Energy Shale Gas Subcommittee's August 2011 draft report on Shale Gas development as an "exceptionally meritorious" mechanism for improving the availability and usefulness of shale gas information among constituencies. According to STRONGER, "the Pennsylvania program is, over all, well-managed, professional and meeting its program objectives." I would go beyond that and say that Pennsylvania has done an exceptional job managing the new challenges that shale gas development presents while allowing our citizens to enjoy the enormous benefits created by this industry.

Pennsylvania does not need federal intervention to ensure an appropriate balance between resource development and environmental protection is struck.

There has been a misconception that the hydraulic fracturing of wells can or has caused contamination of water wells. This is false. First, hydraulic fracturing is only a temporary feature of natural gas development which lasts a few weeks. Hydraulic fracturing of wells is not new in Pennsylvania; it has been going on here since about the 1950s and has been standard practice since about the 1980s. In 2010, the head of EPA's drinking water program, Steve Heare, said that despite claims by environmental organizations, he had not seen any documented cases that the hydro-fracing process was contaminating water supplies. EPA Administrator Lisa Jackson said the exact same thing in her May 24 [2011] testimony before the U.S. House Committee on Oversight and Government Reform. In a January 2010 article in *Platts Gas Daily*, Energy Secretary Stephen Chu said that hydraulic fracturing is safe and lawmakers should be cautious in their efforts to restrict it. My predecessor, former DEP [Department of Environmental Protection] Sec. John Hanger, told Reuters in October 2010 that "Pennsylvania has not had one case in which the fluids used to break off the gas from 5,000 to 8,000 feet underground have returned to contaminate groundwater." Even the limited recent Duke Study of Dimock, Susquehanna County, water samples reports that there was no evidence of fracing fluids in any sample from any of the 68 wells they tested. The study states, "[w]e found no evidence for contamination of drinking-water samples with deep brines or fracturing fluids."

Our ability to unlock the huge clean burning energy source contained in unconventional shale formations will transform Pennsylvania into an energy exporter and move our nation toward energy independence. In addition, we are looking at an economic and energy transformation. We have already seen tens of thousands of new jobs here in Pennsylvania from the industry itself as well as from new industries spawned to support it. These are good paying career jobs in many fields. And that is just the start. There will be hundreds of thousands more good paying skilled and unskilled jobs in a variety of sectors.

While interest in the economic and energy possibilities of the Marcellus is high, my job is to protect public safety and the environment and to do so based on sound science and not fiction or fear. . . .

Pennsylvania's Regulatory Program

Pennsylvania regulates oil and gas well operations under several statutes including the Oil and Gas Act, the Clean Streams Law, the Air Pollution Control Act, the Dam Safety and Encroachments Act and the Solid Waste Management Act. . . . This network of laws and their associated regulations provides the Department of Environmental Protection (DEP) with the tools it needs to comprehensively regulate everything associated with oil and gas development—from locating the well site, site preparation, drilling the well, fresh water withdrawals and water storage, wastewater management, and site restoration.

Simply put, because of our long history of oil and gas development and comprehensive regulatory structure, Pennsylvania does not need federal intervention to ensure an appropriate balance between resource development and environmental protection is struck. . . .

Natural gas holds great promise as a clean burning fuel which could greatly reduce air emissions associated with electricity production and transportation. It has been recognized that combustion of natural gas as either a fuel for generating electricity or a transportation fuel can have very beneficial impacts on air quality. With that being said, Pennsylvania is proactive in minimizing any potential adverse air impacts from extracting this resource.

> *There is no question that states can do and are doing a better job regulating the oil and gas extraction technique of hydraulic fracturing within their borders than the federal government could do.*

Pennsylvania has ample authority under our Pennsylvania Air Pollution Control Act and our air regulations to regulate air emissions from Marcellus Shale gas extraction and processing operations and that is exactly what we do. We focus on minimizing emissions of, for example, nitrogen oxides, carbon monoxide, particulate matter, hazardous air pollutants, and volatile organic compounds (VOC) during the drilling, fracturing, gas collection and processing stages. . . .

Pennsylvania DEP has been very strong on enforcement of rules and regulations in this industry. DEP has shown just this calendar year its agility and decisiveness on the enforcement front in issuing two cease and desist orders as a team within hours when it was appropriate to do so. In one case we issued a "cease drilling order" for non-Marcellus well drilling and in the other case we ordered a stop to pre-drilling well pad preparatory activities which were resulting in sediment being released into a nearby stream upstream of one of the various water intakes of a local water authority. In the latter case we received a letter of thanks from the local water authority for DEP's "immediate" and "prompt response" in doing so. The water authority went on to write "[t]his situation has reinforced our belief that the interest and importance of our water source is of utmost importance to all and that Pennsylvania Department of Environmental Protection works hard to sustain this valuable resource." . . .

No Federal Regulation Is Needed or Justified

There is no question that states can do and are doing a better job regulating the oil and gas extraction technique of hydraulic fracturing within their borders than the federal government could do. No "one size fits all" is applicable in this field. Each state is different and has different geography, topography, geology, hydrogeology and meteorology. In fact, the states in which hydraulic fracturing has and is taking place have been regulating that activity for many years already. The states are light-years ahead of the federal government in terms of experience and know how about their own individual states and about the science and technique of hydraulic fracturing.

It is important to note that federal law going back to the 1970s was never designed or intended to regulate hydraulic fracturing. No federal Congress, no federal President, no federal EPA has ever expressed an interest in a federal regulatory regime for hydraulic fracturing. So one has to ask why the federal government would want to interpose itself here as the states in which hydraulic fracturing is happening are doing a good job doing so and are light-years ahead of the federal EPA on this in terms of time, experience and know-how.

The Marcellus Shale play along with other domestic unconventional resources can transform world energy markets. This potential will only be realized by avoiding the mistakes of the past. Pennsylvania is already showing that the balance of environmental protection and the development of this world-class resource are being accomplished.

10

The Chemicals Used for Fracking Should Be Fully Disclosed

Lisa Song

Lisa Song is a Boston-based reporter for InsideClimate News, a nonprofit, nonpartisan news organization that covers clean energy, carbon energy, nuclear energy, and environmental science with a special focus on where and how law, policy, and public opinion are shaped.

The US Department of Interior's Bureau of Land Management (BLM) oversees some 253 million acres of public lands and 700 million acres of subsurface mineral deposits across the United States. The BLM has recently proposed regulations to require the disclosure of all hydraulic fracking chemicals used in oil and natural gas wells drilled on federal property. The rules would require companies to disclose not just the names of chemicals but also their concentrations within the fracturing fluid. Health advocates and scientists say this information is essential for monitoring air and water quality near drilling sites, responding to emergencies, and ensuring public health. The proposed BLM rules are a positive step toward the mandatory disclosure of dangerous fracking chemicals in all natural gas drilling operations nationwide.

New regulations drafted by the federal Bureau of Land Management would increase pressure on energy companies to disclose information about the chemicals they use in hydraulic fracturing, a process that extracts oil and natural gas from deep inside the earth.

Nine states already have disclosure laws for hydraulic fracturing, also known as fracking. But only one state—Colorado—requires what the BLM would require: the names *and* concentrations of the individual chemicals pumped into each well. Colorado's hotly-contested rules go into effect in April 2012.

Health care professionals and scientists say they need this information to track water and air quality near drilling sites, to study the health effects of natural gas development and to deal with emergency spills.

Proposed Regulations

The proposed BLM regulations, which were leaked to Inside-Climate News and several other media outlets last week [in February 2012], would apply only to wells drilled on federal land. But critics of hydraulic fracturing said they're an important step forward because they're stronger than most state laws.

The agency "should be congratulated," said Theo Colborn, an environmental health analyst who has studied the health effects of natural gas drilling for eight years and has testified before Congress on the need for full industry disclosure. The rules "really begin to reflect the seriousness of the chemicals they're dealing with."

But Colborn and other critics of hydraulic fracturing say there are gaps in the rules that could make them less effective.

Like all the state laws, the BLM would allow companies to exempt certain chemicals or mixtures of compounds that are considered trade secrets. The rules seem to indicate that getting an exemption will be difficult—but how difficult it will be isn't clear. The rules are also unclear about whether companies will be allowed to keep this proprietary information secret from regulators as well as the public.

If you know what's being injected, you'd know what to monitor and track.

The other problem is vague wording about who would have access to the disclosed data. While many states post the information online, the BLM rules don't specify how—or even if—it would make the information available to the public, to health care professionals or to researchers.

Dusty Horwitt, senior counsel at the Environmental Working Group, a nonprofit that advocates for public health, said the trade secret exemptions "could potentially make the rules meaningless if applied broadly."

"If you know what's being injected, you'd know what to monitor and track," Horwitt said. "That would [help] local landowners and scientists. . . . It's also important so officials can make informed decisions about where and how to permit drilling."

A BLM spokesman said he couldn't comment on the proposed rules because they haven't been officially released and may still be changed. He said the official version of the rules will be made available at a later time for public comment.

During hydraulic fracturing, companies pump a mixture of water, sand and fracking products underground at high pressure to increase the flow of gas coming out of a well. The chemical products help break up the rock and release the gas trapped inside.

Hundreds of fracking products are available, some created from a single chemical compound, others from a mixture of chemicals. Although the products make up a tiny fraction (sometimes less than 1 percent by volume) of the total fluid injected during fracking, the overall volumes are so high—up to millions of gallons per well—that a single well often requires thousands of gallons of chemicals.

Those chemicals sometimes include formic acid, which can cause blindness; trimethyl ammonium chloride, which can damage the kidneys and brain, and benzene, which is a known carcinogen.

A single well can be fracked many times, and fracking is now used for 90 percent of the wells drilled in the United States.

Groundwater Contamination

In December, the U.S. Environmental Protection Agency linked fracking to contaminated groundwater in Pavillion, Wyoming. Other scientific studies are under way, but progress has been slow, in part because scientists don't have a complete list of the chemicals they're trying to track.

The rules drafted by the BLM would require companies to report all the products and individual chemicals used at each well, in addition to the chemical concentrations. But the chemicals would not be matched with the products that they go into. The same is true of Colorado's disclosure laws.

Colborn says that's a problem, because if someone is exposed to a particular product, it's important to know the specific chemicals found in that product. The information could help doctors make medical decisions, she said, or guide emergency workers in the event of a spill.

But industry spokespeople say that by keeping the fracking products separate from the individual chemicals they contain, companies can maintain their trade secrets and still allow for public disclosure.

"[It's] just like how you know the ingredients of Coke, but you don't know the exact proportions," said Kathleen Sgamma, vice president of Government and Public Affairs at the industry group Western Energy Alliance. "There's a lot of research and development that goes into the fracking formulas that will work for a particular geology, and that R&D [research and development] needs to be protected. . . . Without that, you don't encourage innovation."

Sgamma said the BLM regulations are unnecessary, because they represent "a top-down federal approach to something that states should and are [already] regulating."

Steve Everley, a spokesman for the industry group Energy in Depth, said that instead of creating new rules, the BLM should use FracFocus, a website set up by regulators and the industry where companies voluntarily post information about the chemicals used in individual wells.

Full disclosure is important for several reasons, including the safety of rig workers and nearby residents.

But critics say voluntary disclosure leaves crucial gaps. Many companies reveal only a fraction of the chemicals they use on FracFocus, and when they label a product "proprietary," they don't offer any indication of its composition.

Everley called the argument for full disclosure a "classic case of moving the goalposts."

"I think the effort itself is being led by people who are against hydraulic fracturing," he said. "It's not about disclosure anymore, it's about some sort of talking point against the industry to paint it in a negative light."

Colborn said full disclosure is important for several reasons, including the safety of rig workers and nearby residents. She is president of the Endocrine Disruption Exchange, a nonprofit in Paonia, Colo., that studies how chemicals in the environment affect public health.

Drilling companies often contract the fracking process to other companies, so rig workers might "have no idea" what they're dealing with, she said. "If they knew what they were using, they wouldn't go out there without respirators and moon suits."

Colborn says local residents also deserve to know what they're being exposed to on a daily basis. A recent ProPublica investigation found that many people who live near drilling rigs complain of headaches, nausea and skin rashes, along with more rare but serious conditions such as cancer. Determining whether their ailments are linked to natural gas development has been difficult, however, because there are few health studies about the impacts of drilling.

The manufacturers of most of the products revealed only a fraction of their chemical makeup.

To adequately monitor air and water quality, scientists "need to use techniques that are designed to look for specific chemicals or specific classes of chemicals," said Robert Howarth, a Cornell University ecology professor who has been deeply involved in the fracking controversy. "This is difficult to do even when we know what is being added. It becomes far more difficult, and far more expensive, when one does not know what you are looking for."

Short-term Tests, Long-term Exposure

Colborn and her colleagues at the Endocrine Disruption Exchange learned firsthand about those research barriers when they set out to survey the health effects of products used in drilling and fracking. Their results were published in September [2011] in the peer-reviewed journal *Human and Ecological Risk Assessment: An International Perspective*.

After more than five years of combing through government and industry reports, they came up with a list of 944 products used at drilling sites. But gaps in data made it impossible for them to evaluate the health impacts of each product.

They discovered that the manufacturers of most of the products revealed only a fraction of their chemical makeup.

Of the 632 chemicals that were revealed, only 353 came with CAS [Chemical Abstracts Service] numbers—the unique codes that the Chemical Abstracts Service (a division of the American Chemical Society) assigns to individual chemical compounds. These codes help scientists and regulators distinguish among different chemicals that share a common name.

CAS numbers are crucial, Colborn said, because chemicals in the same family or class can lead to dramatically different health effects.

Most of the 353 chemicals can affect multiple body systems, the study said. More than 80 percent can damage the skin, eyes and sensory organs, and 52 percent affect the brain and nervous system.

Much of the researchers' information came from Material Safety Data Sheets, because that was the only source of information available. The data sheets are required by the U.S. Occupational Safety and Health Administration and are used to inform workers about the chemicals' dangers and health effects.

Gaps in Information

Michael Wilson, director of UC-Berkeley's Labor Occupational Health Program, said Material Safety Data Sheets are "not at all sufficient for public health decision-making." "They've been plagued for a long time with confidential [and] incomplete information, and virtually no information on long term health and environmental effects."

The industry has not been candid about their practice. . . . Why is it so important to keep [information] from the public?

Aaron Bernstein, a pediatrician and professor at Harvard Medical School, has also studied Material Safety Data Sheets and found them inadequate. He said they may not reveal "whether the chemicals have been tested for potential [health] effects and what they may be."

The subject of testing brings up another challenge. About 80,000 chemicals are registered for use with the EPA, but Colborn said most of them have been tested only for short-term, high dose exposures. Meanwhile, many of the people exposed to natural gas production are experiencing low doses over the long term.

"It would be like putting a new prescription drug on the market only by looking at its effects over a few weeks, when the drug needs to be taken over a lifetime," Bernstein said. "Unfortunately there are people who put chemicals into the environment, and it's entirely legal [to do so] without understanding the potential health risks. And I think fracking is one of them."

"I don't have anything against natural gas per se," Bernstein said. "[But] the industry has not been candid about their practice. . . . Why is it so important to keep [information] from the public?"

Republished with permission of InsideClimate News, a nonprofit, nonpartisan organization that covers energy and climate change—plus the territory in between where law, policy and public opinion are shaped.

11

The Drilling Industry Defends Keeping Fracking Chemicals Secret

Mark Jaffe

Mark Jaffe is a staff writer for The Denver Post *newspaper.*

Natural gas and oil drilling companies fiercely defend keeping the makeup of their individual fracking fluids secret. Making such company trade secrets public, they argue, would give competitors an unfair advantage and could discourage companies from trying innovative chemical technologies that may be effective. Although many companies voluntarily disclose their fracking fluid ingredients on a website called FracFocus.org, they do not necessarily disclose all of them. Industry officials say that even if they do identify all the chemicals in their fracking compounds, they should not have to specify the percentages or concentrations of them because that is proprietary business information. The right to protect trade secrets is protected in both state and federal law, and keeping fracking formulas secret helps drilling companies compete.

Here is the dilemma with the fracking fluids used in oil drilling:

One ingredient found in some of the liquids is aldehyde—which gives cilantro its fragrance and is also in formaldehyde.

While other ingredients in the fluid include more-detailed explanations, when it comes to the aldehyde and some other components of the fluid, that data is simply listed as "Confidential Business Information."

"You'd want to know if they're putting an herb or a poison down an oil well near your house," said Mike Freeman, an attorney with the environmental law group Earthjustice.

The Colorado Oil and Gas Conservation Commission is set to hold a hearing Monday [Dec. 5, 2011,] on a proposed rule requiring disclosure of the chemicals in fracking fluids.

The fluids—which are composed of about 99 percent water and sand—are pumped under pressure down wells to fracture rock and release oil and gas.

The issue is what is in the other 1 percent—which can be as much as 40,000 gallons of chemicals.

The rule would require drillers to file a list of the chemicals and their percentage by volume of the fracking fluid.

The information would be publicly available on an Internet database, FracFocus.org.

A Key Battle

A key battle at Monday's hearing will center on the oil and gas industry's use of "trade secrets" to limit disclosure for some of those ingredients.

"It is a major loophole," said Freeman, who represents five environmental groups in the proceedings, including the Colorado Environmental Coalition.

In comments to the commission, several counties, including Boulder and La Plata, asked that standards be set up to define what qualifies as a trade-secret chemical.

Oil and gas industry executives contend that only a few chemicals are claimed as trade secrets and that their use is crucial to the competitiveness of the industry.

"People are concerned about the groundwater," said state Rep. Marsha Looper, an El Paso County Republican. "So many people depend on wells."

The concern has been heightened by a scramble among drillers to lease mineral rights up and down the front range in a search for oil in the Niobrara formation.

Adequate trade secret protections for hydraulic fracturing chemicals are critically important to ensure that vendors and service providers are not dissuaded from providing or using new and innovative chemical technologies.

In November [2011], Texas-based Anadarko Petroleum Corp. estimated that a section of the Niobrara in Weld County could hold a billion barrels of oil.

But to get at that oil will require horizontally drilled wells and a new and intensive fracking technique that uses 4 million gallons of fluid or more—10 times as much as used in a vertical well.

In comments to the commission, Houston-based Noble Energy, which is drilling oil and gas wells in the Denver-Julesberg Basin, said:

"Adequate trade secret protections for hydraulic fracturing chemicals are critically important to ensure that vendors and service providers are not dissuaded from providing or using new and innovative chemical technologies" in Colorado.

Tulsa-based Williams Cos., a driller on the Western Slope, is proposing that "a balance be struck" so that more chemicals be listed—provided the percentages in the fluid for some are not included.

"This is the ongoing struggle with industry," said Theo Colburn, head of the Endocrine Disruption Exchange—a non-profit group tracking chemicals that have impact on human health. "It is always trying to limit disclosure."

Some companies drilling in Colorado are already voluntarily filing disclosure forms with FracFocus, including Noble and Williams.

A state review of the forms found that trade-secret protection was invoked on 5.8 percent of the chemicals used and that 64 percent of the forms contained no trade-secret chemicals, said David Neslin, oil and gas commission director.

"We assume that hydraulic fracturing fluids are dangerous and should be isolated," he said. "The first line of defense isn't chemical disclosure. It is the integrity of the well and proper handling of the fluid on the surface."

Some fracking fluids had as many as 40 chemicals and 10 proprietary ingredients.

Surface spills and poorly constructed wells that can leak fluid and gas into shallow aquifers pose the greatest risk, Neslin said.

Under Colorado regulations, a well passing through an aquifer must have a metal casing surrounded by a cement jacket, whose integrity has to be documented. During the frack, the job must be monitored by a pressure gauge; if the fracking fluid were to blow out, the pressure would drop.

What Is in It?

A *Denver Post* review of 55 fracking-fluid disclosure sheets on FracFocus for Weld and Garfield counties found an average of 18 ingredients, with two ingredients not disclosed.

The fluids vary based on a range of factors, including geology, depth of well and time of year. Some fracking fluids had as many as 40 chemicals and 10 proprietary ingredients.

There are several ingredients that were often identified on the disclosure forms as proprietary, including:

- Guar gum compound: thickens the water and holds the sand that will keep fractures open. It was as much as 1.6 percent of the fluid.

- Clay stabilizer: prevents clay in the rock formation from swelling and closing cracks or coming loose and clogging pumps. It was about 0.04 percent of the fluid.

- Petroleum distillate: used to reduce friction. It was about 0.003 percent of the fluid.

Guar comes from a bean and is also used as a thickening agent in toothpaste and ice cream.

Staying Ahead of the Competition

For oil-services companies, the key is getting the purest and therefore most effective compound, said Jennifer Miskimins, a petroleum engineering professor at the Colorado School of Mines.

Some clay stabilizers "glue" the clay in places; others absorb the clay—again, the issue is who has the most effective product, she said.

The use of petroleum products—such as diesel oil—in fracking fluids has also been controversial. Miskimins said that lighter petroleum products are more often used because they work better.

The right to trade secrets is protected in both state and federal law, the oil and gas commission's Neslin said. The commission does not have the expertise to evaluate trade secrets, Neslin said, but if there is an accident, spill or signs of pollution, the agency can demand disclosure of the ingredients.

"I'm less worried about what goes down the hole than what comes back up or gets into the air," said the Endocrine Disruption Exchange's Colburn.

12

New Waterless Method Could Reduce Pollution Associated with Fracking

Brian Nearing and Anthony Brino

Brian Nearing is the environmental and science reporter for the Albany Times-Union, *a daily newspaper in Albany, New York. Anthony Brino is a contributor to InsideClimate News, a non-profit, nonpartisan news organization that covers clean energy, carbon energy, nuclear energy, and environmental science with a special focus on where and how law, policy, and public opinion are shaped. The two organizations collaborated to report and jointly publish this viewpoint.*

Fracking is incredibly water-intensive. Massive amounts of water are used to break up shale, and it then returns to the surface as polluted wastewater that must be carefully managed so as not to contaminate drinking water and pollute the environment. A new waterless fracking technology could solve the main environmental problem associated with fracking. Using a liquefied propane gas gel instead of water for fracking has the same fracturing effect on rock, and it effectively frees trapped natural gas. What it does not do is compromise water sources and create a giant pool of contaminated waste. The propane can be recaptured after its use in fracking. Drilling companies have been slow to consider this new technology, however, because propane is more expensive than water, and companies have already heavily invested in hydro-fracking.

In the debate over hydraulic fracturing for natural gas, two facts are beyond dispute: Huge amounts of water are used to break up gas-bearing rock deep underground and huge amounts of polluted water are returned to the surface after the process is complete.

Tainted with chemicals, salts and even mild radioactivity, such water, when mishandled, has damaged the environment and threatened drinking water, helping fuel a heated debate in New York and other states over whether gas drilling is worth its risk to clean drinking water, rivers and streams.

Now, an emerging technology developed in Canada and just making its way to the U.S. does away with the need for water. Instead, it relies on a thick gel made from propane, a widely-available gas used by anyone who has fired up a back-yard barbecue grill.

Gas Fracking

Called liquefied propane gas (LPG) fracturing, or simply "gas fracking," the waterless method was developed by a small Canadian energy company, GasFrac, based in Calgary, Alberta.

Still awaiting a patent in the U.S., the technique has been used about 1,000 times since 2008, mainly in gas wells in the Canadian provinces of Alberta, British Columbia and New Brunswick and a smaller handful of test wells in states that include Texas, Pennsylvania, Colorado, Oklahoma and New Mexico, said GasFrac Chief Technology Officer Robert Lestz.

Like water, propane gel is pumped into deep shale formations a mile or more underground, creating immense pressure that cracks rocks to free trapped natural gas bubbles. Like water, the gel also carries small particles of sand or man-made material—known as proppant—that are forced into cracks to hold them open so the gas can flow out.

Unlike water, the gel does a kind of disappearing act underground. It reverts to vapor due to pressure and heat, then returns to the surface—along with the natural gas—for collection, possible reuse and ultimate resale.

And also unlike water, propane does not carry back to the surface drilling chemicals, ancient seabed salts and underground radioactivity.

Using gas instead of water can serve two ends—protecting the environment and reducing costs to the drilling industry.

"We leave the nasties in the ground, where they belong," said Lestz.

David Burnett, a professor of petroleum engineering at Texas A&M University, one of the nation's premier petroleum engineering schools, said fracking with propane makes sense.

"From a reservoir engineering perspective, there is no reason this would not be effective," said Burnett, who runs the Environmentally Friendly Drilling Systems Program, a project of the university and the Houston Advanced Research Center, a not-for-profit academic and business consortium. Supported by some of the nation's largest energy companies, as well as by the New York State Energy Research and Development Authority, the drilling program seeks new technologies that develop gas and oil in a safe and environmentally friendly manner.

Burnett said using gas instead of water can serve two ends—protecting the environment and reducing costs to the drilling industry of handling and disposing of tainted water.

But he said propane fracturing is "not a game changer," at least not yet.

"This is a very conservative industry," Burnett said. "Engineers want to see what someone else did first, and they want the data." Most companies that have tried the GasFrac technique have not published data publicly, he said, possibly out of fear of tipping off potential competitors to its benefits.

A search of public research reports on file with the Society of Petroleum Engineers found only two case studies for wells that used propane fracking—one in 2011 and one in 2009. "You are going to need more than one or two wells to prove this to the industry," Burnett said. And because gas fracking is a proprietary method owned by a still small company with limited ability to supply and service many new users, "if more people want to use the technology, the cost will probably go up. So GasFrac is kind of caught in a Catch-22."

Still in Its Infancy

Propane fracking is still in its infancy, and only time will tell whether the technique will make inroads in a global drilling industry that began using water-based fracking in the late 1940s and since has invested vast amounts in that technology. Hydrofracking for natural gas is now used in more than a dozen states, Canada and around the world. "The infrastructure is already there for water, people have already put millions into it," Lestz said. "Sometimes the good is the enemy of the great."

Wells now have 20 propane sensors, up from three, as well as an infrared video monitor that allows gas leaks to be seen by well crews.

Aside from being better environmentally, Lestz said propane fracking also can be more efficient, because it allows more gas to flow from wells than water-based fracturing. All the propane leaves the fractured rocks, unlike water, part of which remains behind and can be absorbed into rock to partially block the pathways for gas to escape.

Also, the propane method uses only about one quarter of the number of truck trips that water-based fracking employs, so the impact on local roads, the noise and dust annoyance to neighbors, and the trucking costs for drillers are reduced, he said.

However, propane costs more initially to use, even though it can be resold once recovered. It is also explosive, and requires special equipment to be handled properly and reduce risk.

In January [2011], there was a flash fire at an LPG gas well being drilled in Alberta by Husky Energy, one of Canada's largest energy companies and one of the first to embrace LPG drilling. Three workers suffered burns, although no injuries were life-threatening.

Lestz said an undetected propane leak was to blame, and the company subsequently added more monitoring equipment to reduce the risks. Wells now have 20 propane sensors, up from three, as well as an infrared video monitor that allows gas leaks to be seen by well crews.

A spokesman for the Alberta Department of Occupational Health and Safety said the mishap is still being investigated.

A spokesman from Husky declined questions, saying the company did not want to get "dragged into" any debate about gas drilling.

However, in September, Husky gave GasFrac a vote of confidence with a new three-year contract that carries a two-year renewal option.

And a month before that, the company obtained $100 million in funding from HSBC Bank Canada, Bank of Montreal and Alberta Treasury Branches to help it grow. Lestz said Gas-Frac expects to be able to expand its equipment "fleet" from two in 2010 to a dozen by 2012.

An industry executive with ties to New York said propane's expense does make it a tough sell. "Propane is always going to be more expensive than water," said Roger Willis, president of Universal Well Services, a Pennsylvania company that provides drilling equipment to the industry. "But propane fracking will probably be useful in some situations. . . . The economics of doing it would be fairly complicated. You have to weigh the cost and recovery of propane versus the transport and treatment of the water."

Fracking in New York

The New York Oil & Gas Association, a lobbying group, referred a reporter to Willis after being asked for the group's stance on propane fracking.

New York is anticipating allowing "produced" water to be taken by municipal sewer treatment plants that have been retrofitted and approved by the state to properly handle drilling contaminants. However, no plants in the state currently have that approval.

How to safely transport and dispose of millions of gallons of produced wastewater is one of the issues being wrestled with as the New York Department of Environmental Conservation considers opening up the state to hydrofracking.

The state expects between 1,600 and 2,500 gas wells a year eventually could be hydrofracked in the gas-rich Marcellus Shale, an underground formation that runs from the western Catskills, and through the Finger Lakes and Southern Tier almost to Buffalo, and runs south through Pennsylvania and West Virginia.

An average well can use up to 7.8 million gallons of water; about a fifth of it returns to the surface and requires disposal. So, that could be billions of gallons of well water that has to be trucked in and trucked out for disposal elsewhere.

[Liquid propane gas] technology is proprietary to Gas-Frac, and so has limited availability.

Propane fracturing is emerging just as New York tries to avoid repeating water disposal problems seen in Pennsylvania, where used well water taken to regular sewer treatment plants ended up fouling rivers in the western part of the state—including the Allegheny River, source of some of Pittsburgh's drinking water.

This spring [2011], Pennsylvania officials found that high levels of bromides in treated drilling wastewater were being altered by the chlorine-based sewage treatment into a carcinogen. The state asked drilling companies to voluntarily stop taking drilling wastewater to more than a dozen treatment plants.

New York's Department of Environmental Conservation [DEC] devoted a few paragraphs to propane fracking in its 1,500-page Draft Generic Environmental Impact Statement report on natural gas drilling in September [2011]. It tersely declared that the technology was "not mature enough" to support drilling in New York.

As well as costing more than water, the LPG technology is proprietary to GasFrac, and so has limited availability, the DEC said.

But the agency also seemed to recognize the technology's potential, adding: "While it is not known if or when LPG hydraulic fracturing will be proposed in New York, having ... infrastructure in place may be an important factor in realizing the advantages of this technology."

New York would appear to have a ready source of propane available for fracking, as a major propane pipeline runs from Pennsylvania through the heart of the Marcellus Shale area in the Southern Tier. The Teppco pipeline goes through Watkins Glen, Oneonta and Selkirk before continuing into New England.

"This technology will be 'mature' in our view when we have a proposal or an application to review," DEC spokeswoman Charsleissa King said. "At this point we do not have anything before us. We have met with GasFrac to get a general understanding of the technology."

Going Mainstream

Lestz admits his company does not have nearly enough equipment to take its method mainstream. He said it envisions forming "strategic alliances" with larger, unidentified drilling companies to make its process more available.

"New York is very important. No companies there have put their cards on the table, so it is still virgin territory," said Lestz, who has traveled twice to New York to tout propane fracking.

Two independent gas drilling companies that have run LPG wells—one outside of Moncton, New Brunswick, a few hours north of the Maine border, and another in Maverick County, Texas, close to Rio Grande River and Mexico—said they found the technique to be promising.

Since 2008 30 LPG wells have been drilled in British Columbia, all by GasFrac.

Calgary-based Jadela Oil drilled a well in Texas using Gas-Frac equipment in August. Company president Greg Lee said initial results showed gas flowing, and the well is now "shut-in" to allow pressure to build so gas can be collected.

"My gut feeling is that this is the way to go," said Lee. He said LPG can make gas wells more productive by eliminating potential blockage by water left behind and absorbed into fractured rock, which can close off some pathways for trapped gas to rise.

Lee says that while propane must be handled with care, hydraulic fracturing also has risks. Lee advocates greater industry attention to risks in fracking.

Data Are Hard to Find

Burnett, from the environmentally-friendly drilling program at Texas A&M, said his group has been trying, so far unsuccessfully, to get Jadela's data on its propane gas well. "This is the kind of technology that our group is trying to locate, to document and then make that information available to the industry."

Phillip Knoll, president of Nova Scotia–based Corridor Resources, said his company started drilling propane wells in 2009 in New Brunswick, west of Moncton. His company released a 2011 case study available through the Society of Petroleum Engineers. It showed gas fracking can work.

"We had absolutely tremendous results that compared favorably with other techniques," like hydrofracking, said Knoll. "This technology is improving substantially."

His company also uses water-based hydrofracking.

Since 2008 30 LPG wells have been drilled in British Columbia, all by GasFrac, said Sandra Steilo, a spokeswoman for the Ministry of Energy and Mines. No accidents have been reported.

She offered an explanation for why the LPG method is not more widely used. "As far as we're aware, the technology has so far not proved cost-effective for gas wells," she said. "The technology works best when sufficient infrastructure is in place to allow the propane to be captured and re-used."

Organizations to Contact

The editors have compiled the following list of organizations concerned with the issues debated in this book. The descriptions are derived from materials provided by the organizations. All have publications or information available for interested readers. The list was compiled on the date of publication of the present volume; names, addresses, phone and fax numbers, and e-mail and Internet addresses may change. Be aware that many organizations take several weeks or longer to respond to inquiries, so allow as much time as possible.

American Petroleum Institute (API)
1220 L St. NW, Washington, DC   20005-4070
(202) 682-8000
website: www.energyfromshale.org

The American Petroleum Institute is the national trade association for the oil and natural gas industry. API represents producers, refiners, suppliers, pipeline operators, and transporters, as well as service and supply companies that support all segments of the industry. API speaks for the petroleum industry to the public, federal and state governments, and the media. The organization maintains a website devoted to hydraulic fracturing called EnergyFromShale.org. The site features explanations of the fracking process, descriptions of the major natural gas plays in the United States, information about the challenges the industry faces, and news items related to the natural gas industry. Numerous reports can be downloaded from the site, including "The Hydraulic Fracturing Primer—Freeing Up Energy" and "Are We Entering the Golden Age of Gas?"

America's Natural Gas Alliance (ANGA)
701 Eighth St. NW, Suite 800, Washington, DC   20001
(202) 789-2642
e-mail: info@anga.us
website: www.anga.us

America's Natural Gas Alliance represents thirty of North America's largest independent natural gas exploration and production companies. ANGA works to promote the economic, environmental, and national security benefits of the increased use of domestic natural gas. The ANGA website offers extensive information about natural gas exploration and extraction, including a downloadable primer on fracking, titled "Hydraulic Fracturing 101." The site also features an extensive video library on natural gas topics; its *Natural Gas Now* video series includes the titles "Voices of the Shale," "Clean Energy from Coast to Coast," and "Clean Energy Jobs," all of which can be viewed on the site.

Chesapeake Energy Corporation
PO Box 18496, Oklahoma City, OK   73154-0496
(405) 935-8000
e-mail: info@hydraulicfracturing.com
website: www.hydraulicfracturing.com

Cheseapeake Energy Corporation, one of the world's largest extractors of natural gas, maintains a website devoted to hydraulic fracturing. HydraulicFracturing.com features in-depth explanations of the fracking process, detailed descriptions of the major natural gas sites in the United States, information about Cheseapeake's Green Frac initiative, a FAQ that includes a list of common fracking fluid ingredients and their uses, and an extensive collection of links to external resources, such as congressional testimony, research studies, and government reports.

Food & Water Watch
1616 P St. NW, Suite 300, Washington, DC   20036
(202) 683-2500 • fax: (202) 683-2501
e-mail: info@fwwatch.org
website: www.foodandwaterwatch.org

Founded in 2005, Food & Water Watch is a nonprofit organization that advocates for commonsense policies that will result in healthy, safe food and access to safe and affordable drinking water. The group believes that it is essential for shared resources to be regulated in the public interest rather than for private gain, and one of its top priorities is to ban hydraulic fracturing. The organization's website offers extensive content related to fracking, including issue briefs, fact sheets, and reports with titles such as "Fracking and the Food System," "Waste: The Soft and Dirty Underbelly of Fracking," and "Fracking: The New Global Water Crisis." An "Action Center" area of the site offers suggestions and opportunities for getting involved in the antifracking effort.

FracFocus
Ground Water Protection Council, 13308 N. MacArthur Blvd.
Oklahoma City, OK   73142
(405) 516-4972
e-mail: info@gwpc.org
website: www.fracfocus.org

The FracFocus website is an online registry for the voluntary disclosure of hydraulic fracturing chemicals used in oil and natural gas extraction. The website is a joint project of the Ground Water Protection Council and the Interstate Oil and Gas Compact Commission. Site visitors can search for wells by state to find information about the chemicals used in the hydraulic fracturing of those wells. FracFocus has recorded over fifteen thousand disclosures from more than 230 participating companies. The site also offers a variety of downloadable reports related to the fracking process, groundwater protection, chemical use, and state regulations, and site visitors can submit questions or comments from the "Ask a Question" page.

Gasland
e-mail: shixson@newvideo.com
website: www.gaslandthemovie.com

The official site for the documentary film *Gasland* features reviews, clips, and trailers from the movie, FAQs about fracking, information about the FRAC Act, an interactive map of gaslands in the United States, and suggestions for antifracking activism. Available for download from the site is "Affirming *Gasland*," director Josh Fox's detailed point-by-point response to the natural gas industry's challenges to the information presented in his movie. Visitors can sign up for political action alerts, and the "Take Action" section of the site invites people to share their experiences with hydrofracking via a "Share Your Story" online form. Fox plans to deliver the collected testimonies to Congress.

Natural Resources Defense Council (NRDC)
40 W. Twentieth St., New York, NY   10011
(212) 727-2700 • fax: (212) 727-1773
e-mail: nrdcinfo@nrdc.org
website: www.nrdc.org

The Natural Resources Defense Council promotes the international protection of wildlife and wild places through law, science, and a membership of over 1 million people. Some of the main priorities of the organization include reducing global temperatures, developing alternative technologies for energy, and protecting the world's oceans and endangered habitats. The NRDC opposes fracking until effective safeguards are in place, and it offers a variety of news and informational resources related to fracking via its website. Resources available include the NRDC issue briefs and reports "Risky Gas Drilling Threatens Health, Water Supplies," "Don't Get Fracked! Steps to Keep You and Your Family Safe from Drilling," and "Fracking, Natural Gas, Water Pollution."

US Senate Committee on Energy and Natural Resources
304 Dirksen Senate Bldg., Washington, DC   20510
(202) 224-4971 • fax: (202) 224-6163
website: www.energy.senate.gov

The US Senate Committee on Energy and Natural Resources is the congressional body that has jurisdiction over matters related to energy and public lands. Its far-reaching legislative activity covers energy resources and development; regulation and conservation; strategic petroleum reserves; public lands and their renewable resources; surface mining; federal coal, oil, gas, and other mineral leasing; and water resources. Full transcripts for testimony related to natural gas production and fracking can be found by searching the committee's website.

Bibliography

Books

Canadian Association of Energy and Pipeline Landowner Associations (CAEPLA)

A Revolution Underground: The History, Economics and Environmental Impacts of Hydraulic Fracturing. Calgary, AB: CAEPLA, 2012.

Carrie Fredericks

Fueling the Future: Natural Gas. Detroit: Greenhaven Press, 2007.

Abrahm Lustgarten

Hydrofracked? One Man's Mystery Leads to a Backlash Against Natural Gas Drilling. New York: ProPublica, 2011.

Seamus McGraw

The End of Country: Dispatches from the Frack Zone. New York: Random House, 2011.

Tara Meixsell

Collateral Damage: A Chronicle of Lives Devastated by Gas and Oil Development and the Valiant Grassroots Fight to Effect Political and Legislative Change. Seattle: CreateSpace, 2010.

Alex Prud'homme

The Ripple Effect: The Fate of Fresh Water in the Twenty-First Century. New York: Scribner, 2011.

Peter Ralph

Dirty Fracking Business. Melbourne, Australia: Melbourne Books, 2012.

United States Department of Energy	*Modern Shale Gas Development in the United States: A Primer.* N.p.: Progressive Management, 2011.
United States Environmental Protection Agency	*21st Century Guide to Hydraulic Fracturing.* N.p.: Progressive Management, 2010.
United States Geological Survey	*2012 Guide to Natural Gas Hydraulic Fracturing from Shale Formations.* N.p.: Progressive Management, 2011.
David Waples	*The Natural Gas Industry in Appalachia: A History from the First Discovery to the Tapping of the Marcellus Shale.* Jefferson, NC: McFarland, 2012.
Tom Wilber	*Under the Surface: Fracking, Fortunes, and the Fate of the Marcellus Shale.* Ithaca, NY: Cornell University Press, 2012.

Periodicals and Internet Sources

Ronald Bailey	"Natural Gas Flip-Flop: Big Environmental Groups Were for Fracking Before They Were Against It," *Reason*, August/September 2011.
Neela Banerjee	"'Gasland' Director Joshua Fox Arrested Filming House Panel," *Los Angeles Times*, February 1, 2012.

David Biello   "What the Frack? Natural Gas from Subterranean Shale Promises U.S. Energy Independence—with Environmental Costs," *Scientific American*, March 30, 2010.

Bipartisan Policy Center Energy Project   "Shale Gas: New Opportunities, New Challenges," Bipartisan Policy Center, January 2012. http://bipartisanpolicy.org.

Mark Clayton   "EPA to Natural Gas Companies: Give Details on 'Fracking' Chemicals," *Christian Science Monitor*, September 9, 2010.

Lauren Donovan   "Some Companies Disclose Fracking Chemical Recipes," *Bismark (ND) Tribune*, November 27, 2011.

Nicole Weisensee Egan   "Living with 'Fracking': Where the Water Catches Fire," *People*, February 6, 2012.

Lena Groeger   "Federal Rules to Disclose Fracking Chemicals Could Come with Exceptions," ProPublica, February 16, 2012. www.propublica.org.

Nicholas Kusnetz   "North Dakota's Oil Boom Brings Damage Along with Prosperity," ProPublica, June 7, 2012. www.propublica.org.

Marc Levy   "PA: No Red Flags over Radioactivity in 7 Rivers," *Washington Post*, March 7, 2011.

Abrahm Lustgarten	"Injection Wells: The Poison Beneath Us," *Mother Jones*, June 26, 2012.
Michael Mishak	"Mystery of Fracking Chemicals Worries Californians," *Los Angeles Times*, March 19, 2012.
Mother Nature Network	"Exxon Defends Fracking Techniques," May 29, 2011. www.mnn.com.
National Petroleum Council	"Prudent Development: Realizing the Potential of North America's Abundant Natural Gas and Oil Resources," *Crude Oil and Natural Gas Resources and Supply*, September 15, 2011.
Joe Nocera	"How to Extract Gas Responsibly," *New York Times*, February 27, 2012.
Stephen Osborn et al.	"Methane Contamination of Drinking Water Accompanying Gas-Well Drilling and Hydraulic Fracturing," ProPublica, April 14, 2011. www.propublica.org.
Andrew Revkin	"More Views on the Gas Rush and Hydraulic Fracturing," *New York Times*, July 2, 2012.
Kate Sheppard	"For Pennsylvania's Doctors, a Gag Order on Fracking Chemicals," *Mother Jones*, March 23, 2012.
Mike Soraghan	"EPA Looking for Ways to 'Manage or Minimize' Injection Earthquakes," *EnergyWire*, March 15, 2012. www.eenews.net.

Elizabeth Souder   "Exxon CEO Defends Natural Gas Drilling Against Activists' Warnings," *Dallas Morning News*, May 25, 2011.

Alex Trembath   "US Government Role in Shale Gas Fracking History: An Overview and Response to Our Critics," Breakthrough Institute, March 12, 2012. http://thebreakthrough.org.

Ian Urbina   "Drilling Down, Part 1: Regulation Lax as Gas Wells' Tainted Water Hits Rivers," *New York Times*, February 26, 2011.

Ian Urbina   "Drilling Down, Part 2: Wastewater Recycling No Cure-All in Gas Process," *New York Times*, March 2, 2011.

Ian Urbina   "Drilling Down, Part 3: Pressure Limits Efforts to Police Drilling for Gas," *New York Times*, March 3, 2011.

Bryan Walsh   "The Golden Age: Could Europe and China's Fracking Forays Remake Global Energy?," *Time*, May 21, 2012.

Alyson Warhit   "Study: Fracking May Be More Harmful than Coal Use," *Cornell University Daily Sun*, April 18, 2011.

Ben Wolfgang   "Earthquake Link Casts Cloud over Fracking," *Washington Times*, March 12, 2012.

Fareed Zakaria   "The Game-Changer in the
                      Geopolitics of Energy," *GPS* (blog),
                      CNN.com, June 10, 2012.
                      http://globalpublicsquare.blogs.cnn.com.

Fareed Zakaria   "Natural Gas Fueling an Economic
                      Revolution," *Washignton Post*, March
                      29, 2012.

Index

A

Air pollution
    fracking risk, 12–13, 33–36, 66
    importance of, 34–36
    overview, 33–34
    protection from, 17
    reduction of, 15
    Texas study on, 36
Air Pollution Control Act, 65
Air quality protection, 14, 16
Aldehyde liquid, 76–77
American Petroleum Institute, 21,
    35, 59–60
Anadarko Petroleum Corp., 78
Antifracking legislation, 8
Arsenic, 13, 47

B

Benzene, 9, 13, 30, 35–36, 71
Bernstein, Aaron, 74–75
Bloomberg News, 8, 57–58
Boling, Mark, 58, 60
Bromides, 47–48, 87
Bulgaria, 8

C

Cabot Oil & Gas Corp. (COG), 60
Canada, 21, 25, 82, 84–85
Carcinogens (cancer-causing
    chemicals)
    arsenic, 13, 47
    benzene, 9, 13, 30, 35–36, 71
    bromides, 47–48, 87
    diesel oil, 9, 80

ethylbenzene, 9
formaldehyde, 9, 76
in fracking fluid, 23
naphthalene, 9
tests for, 30
toluene, 9
trimethyl ammonium chlo-
    ride, 74
2-butoxyethanol (2-BE), 9, 32
xylene, 9
Chemical Abstracts Service (CAS),
    74
Chemical concerns with fracking
    chlorine, 48, 71, 87
    competition concerns, 80
    drilling industry won't reveal,
        76–80
    formic acid, 71
    glycol ethers, 28
    groundwater contamination,
        64, 71–73
    information gaps, 74–75
    key battle over, 77–79
    overview, 69, 76–77
    proposed regulations of,
        69–71
    public disclosure needs, 16,
        68–75
    short-term tests and long-
        term exposure, 73–74
    types of chemicals used,
        79–80
    See also Carcinogens; Methane
        contamination
Cheney, Dick, 9
Chesapeake Energy Corp. (CHK),
    59
China, 25